HOW-TO-GROW
WORLD CLASS
GIANT
PUMPKINS, II

A world class book for anyone who grows giant pumpkins with world record aspirations!

by Don Langevin

05155I

A continuation of the classic book on growing giant pumpkins,
How-to-Grow World Class Giant Pumpkins,
Annedawn Publishing, Box 247, Norton, MA 02766

Annedawn Publishing
Box 247, Norton, MA 02766
508-222-9069

Copyright © 1998 by Donald G. Langevin
First Printing 1998
Printed in the United States of America
Library of Congress Cataloging in Publication Data
Langevin, Donald G.
How-to-Grow World Class Giant Pumpkins II / Don Langevin
1st edition.
Library of Congress Catalog Card Number: 98-71390

ISBN 0-9632793-5-1

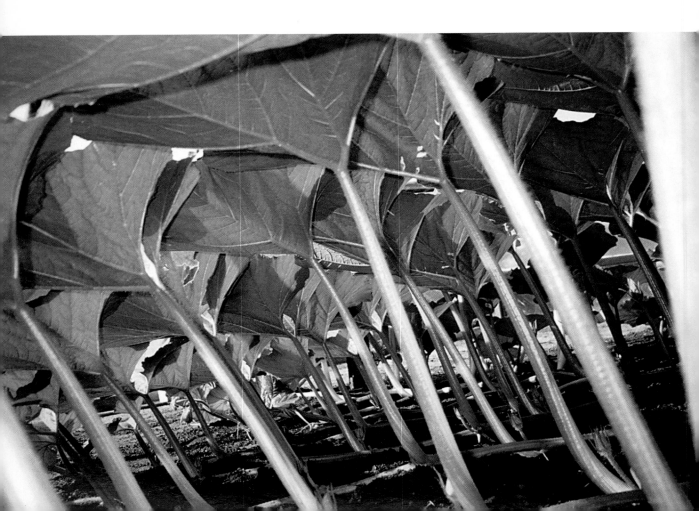

Dedication

For John Castellucci, who never stopped telling me, "You should write!"

Acknowledgements

I am indebted to anyone who has ever put a giant pumpkin seed into the ground with the hope of growing a fruit that could be enjoyed by others. Whether you grow for the fun of it, for bragging rights in your family or neighborhood, or you are totally committed to growing a genuine world class giant pumpkin, your enthusiasm for the sport was the reason why I began writing about giant pumpkins in the first place.

In writing both, *How-to-Grow World Class Giant Pumpkins* and this sequel, I was constantly assisted by top growers, weigh off site coordinators, association newsletter editors and my closest giant-pumpkin-growing friends: John Castellucci, Ron and Dick Wallace and Tim Donovan. Without the support and encouragement of these people, there would have been no motivation to write another book on this subject.

Without the assistance and generosity of the following people, the fine pictures, biographical and cultural information, and data contained within these pages would not have been possible. These fine people have given much to the sport of giant pumpkin growing without expecting anything in return: Chris Andersen, Herman Bax, Al and Yvette Berard, Jan Bonhomme, Glen Brown, John Castellucci, Tony Ciliberto, Warren Cole, Steve Connolly, Barry DeJong, Howard and Danny Dill, Al Eaton, Del Edwards, Geneva and Don Emmons, David Ferro, Maribeth Fitts, Alan Gibson, Pete Glasier, Bill Greer, Wayne Hackney, Dave Hampton, Joel and Mari Lou Holland, Gary Keyzer, Brian Kitney, Jim Kuhn, Jack and Sherry LaRue, George and Deanna Lloyd, Bob Marcellus, Duncan McAlpine, Paula McGeary, Joe Mills, Ann Molloy, Kirk Mombert, Lorraine Orr, Bob and Utoni Ruff, Gus and Joan Saunders, Chris Servant, Phillip Simpson, John Snyder, Dave Stelts, Dave, Ron and Dick Wallace, Ray Waterman (World Pumpkin Confederation), Craig Weir, Hugh and Barbara Wiberg and Dr. Robert Wick.

Finally, I must give the greatest gift of acknowledgement to my mother, Mae Lachance. She has steadfastly loved and unconditionally supported me for over fifty years now. A single act of motherly kindness she made in 1992 created for me a new path of life to walk down. Not willing to make an investment in myself, she stepped forward to make, what seems today to have been an insignificant decision, but then was a supreme act of love and confidence in her son. Her purchase of a $700, Macintosh Classic computer for my birthday opened a new door for me and set me on the way to writing and self-publishing books. It not only gave me the opportunity to be more productive and to earn more for my family, it introduced me to a new career (at age 44) in electronic graphic arts and desktop publishing. If not for this gift, I would never have had the opportunity to discover and explore talents that I never knew existed but for which she had always seen.

Contents

Foreword		**7**
Introduction		**9**
Chapter 1	**The Heavy Hitters**	**13**
Chapter 2	**Seeds and Sources**	**45**
Chapter 3	**Family Trees**	**49**
Chapter 4	**Sun and Soil**	**53**
Chapter 5	**Seed Starting**	**59**
Chapter 6	**Planting and Early Season Protection**	**63**
Chapter 7	**Feeding and Watering**	**69**
Chapter 8	**Pollination**	**77**

Chapter 9	Fruit Selection	83
Chapter 10	Training, Pruning & Fruit Protection	87
Chapter 11	Insidious Insects & Demon Diseases	95
Chapter 12	Critter Control	107
Chapter 13	Estimating Weight	111
Chapter 14	Murphy's Law	117
Chapter 15	Late Protection	123
Chapter 16	Competing and Having Fun	127
Chapter 17	What do you do with that?	137
Chapter 18	World Class Sites & Associations	149
Appendix		155

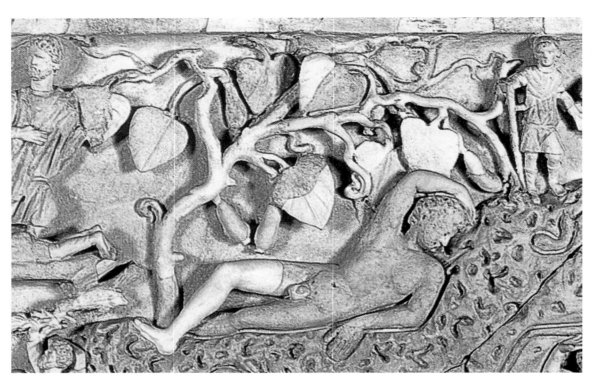

6 And the LORD God prepared a [2] gourd, and made *it* to come up over Jonah, that it might be a shadow over his head, to deliver him from his grief. So Jonah [3] was exceeding glad of the gourd.

7 But God prepared a worm when the morning rose the next day, and it smote the gourd that it withered.

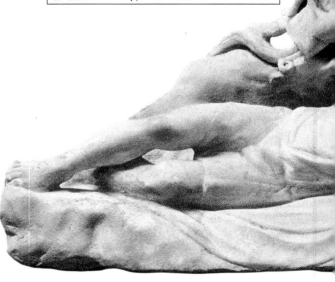

Bible quote is from the book of Jonah (Chapter 4, Verses 4-6).

Top: 3rd century relief sculpture on sarcophagus in Vatican, Rome cemetery depicting cycle of Jonah.

To right: 3rd century marble sculpture from the Eastern Mediterranean titled Jonah Beneath the Castor-Oil Plant (Cleveland Museum of Art).

Foreword

Man's quest has been an amazing journey. We've seen great and wonderful happenings related to the achievements of mankind. But when a quest becomes the challenge, and records become the goal, even greater things happen. Who would ever think that growing a pumpkin would present such a demand of one's absolute best effort? This sport/hobby has become a worldwide passion and Don Langevin's sequel tells it best!

The quest for the world's first 1,000 lb. pumpkin had been likened to accomplishments such as: running the first four minute mile, conquering Mt. Everest, or putting a man on the moon! Only if you've selected an *Atlantic Giant* pumpkin seed and dreamed of harvest's glory can you rightfully consider this kinship. Attaining the 1,000 lb. challenge was a ten year commitment by many of the world's best growers. In 1984 the World Pumpkin Confederation offered a $10,000 prize for the USA's first 500-pounder. A 600-pounder was grown and we were off to the races. In 1986 the confederation first promoted the 1,000 lb. challenge. After ten years, and prizes of $25,000 and later $50,000, the race had been won! Where do we take this phenomenon — man's quest for the largest? You see, this is about much more than growing a few pumpkins. This is about humanity; you and me accepting our personal and united challenge to grow the world's largest pumpkin. How big can they get? The 1,500 lb. mark is now identified.

Much of the awareness the sport/hobby has attained is due to the media pronouncing the annual world winner. Everyone wants to know about the biggest pumpkin — it's only natural! This book, however, is a concise report of the sport/hobby itself. Not any different than any other sport or hobby, giant pumpkin growing has its hopes and aspirations and they can all be found here. Absolutely the best "how-to" book for growing giant pumpkins!

In these pages you will visit some of the world's best growers and see their accomplishments. From all walks of life, some young and some old; a few are new to the challenge and many are seasoned gardeners with serious giant pumpkin credentials. And if its keeping a young grower's interest focused, or providing the drive for a senior to keep "growing," it all falls into play with the early objective this sport/hobby was founded upon. You see, there are no real limitations for mankind; if we can put our best effort forth in a formula for competitive gardening success (and life for that matter) which involves: 1. Gain experience with the variety and understand it. 2. Deter any negative influences. 3. Enhance positive conditions and situations. 4. Set goals. And 5. Achieve. Using this formula, combined with a few prayers, you can be a great grower as well.

Ray Waterman
President and Founder
World Pumpkin Confederation

Dick and Ron Wallace (far left and second from left) measure their 1997, 628.2-pound pumpkin with John Castellucci just prior to harvest. Far right: Don Langevin records measurements.

Introduction

I have thought about this book for some time, mainly because the readers of my first book on pumpkins, *How-to-Grow World Class Giant Pumpkins,* would not stop asking the question, "When will you write another book on giant pumpkins?" I must apologize because I was falling into the same trap that I had seen others take when I began researching my first book. One top grower and respected organizer, who I had solicited information from, had told me, "Why would anyone want to write a book on pumpkin growing when everything that can be said about the subject has already been written?" At the time this infuriated me because I knew of no one who had presented a concise description, from A to Z, on the subject; and no one had ever published color photos of famous giant pumpkins. I ignored the comment and eight months later published the first complete text with color photos on the subject. From the very start it was a smash hit among gardeners. Even the most staid, competitive giant pumpkin growers called it, "Long overdue."

Later, friends and fellow competitors testified that the book had finally put them on a level playing field with the hundred, or so, successful growers back in 1993. For once, a person with good gardening skills could compete with the top echelon growers of the world. I don't want you to think that I'm taking all the credit for this, because I am emphatically not. The *Dill's Atlantic Giant* pumpkin variety is the great equalizer among giant pumpkin growers. Anyone with this seed has the chance to compete on a world class level. My book merely pointed this out and harnessed the energy of this seed variety for the novice or inexperienced grower. There are no tricks or smoke and mirrors, but there are some generally accepted cultural methods in growing giant pumpkins that I feel are pretty widespread now because of my first book. *How-to-Grow World Class Giant Pumpkins* helped thousands of backyard growers to become competitive in the sport of giant pumpkin growing.

So, how did I escape the trap of thinking everything had been written? I, plain and simple, started to look around at what was occurring. The 1000-pound barrier was broken. The yardstick by which we measure world class had

Pumpkins and squash are proudly displayed at the WPC, weigh off in Collins, NY. Collins is considered to be the mecca of giant vegetable growing in North America with competitions in many categories.

been raised to above 900 pounds — 900-pound pumpkins are becoming commonplace. Joel Holland's, 1993, world record, 827 would not have finished in the top twelve in 1997. In almost every top weigh off site in North America between the 40th and 46th parallels in 1997, it took an 800-pound pumpkin to break into the select group of top growers for that site. First and second year growers are growing, routinely, 500-700-pound pumpkins. The cast of top growers has changed almost yearly with many new faces entering since 1993. The *Heavy Hitters* still do remarkably well, but there is just so much more competition now, it takes a super human effort, and an enormous amount of luck, to become a world champion.

How people grow giant pumpkins has been maturing. There still is much that is theorized, and many different methods are chosen, but the bulk of information has begun to solidify, and more and more facets of growing giants are now becoming gospel. *How-to-Grow World Class Giant Pumpkins, II* had to be written to further educate growers who have few contacts in the sport, and grow more for the fun of it, than for the competition. This book attempts to bring those that have read my first book, "up to speed" on every facet of growing a world record pumpkin. I still consider my first book required reading for anyone with aspirations of being a world champion. Some things never change, and many of those things are covered in my first book, and will not be covered here. Nonetheless, I have attempted to cover everything about growing from seed to harvest in this sequel so that a first-time reader of mine can garner valuable information that can contribute to their success. This book will introduce new concepts, new methods and new ways of looking at the growing of giant pumpkins and the sport. It will certainly make you a better grower by exposing you, at times, to some "heady" dissertation on the subject. Bear with me, because as you become more enthralled with the sport, you will begin to explore many of the avenues that are travelled in this sequel.

Don Langevin

chapter one

The Heavy Hitters

When it comes to growing world class giant pumpkins, these growers are the very best — from the Eastern Maritime of Canada to the Pacific Northwest of the United States.

There are many growers who are deserving of the distinction of *Heavy Hitter,* and therefore, it was not easy choosing those who are presented here. About a hundred growers were considered for the distinction, and in the final analysis, it came down to sheer weight as the most important factor — after all, this is not a beauty contest. In my first book, *How-to-Grow World Class Giant Pumpkins,* a great deal of attention was paid to people who contribute to the well-being of the sport. Very little of that occurs here, but it is nice to report, that all of the *Heavy Hitters* in this edition are role models for new growers based on their willingness to help anyone sincerely interested in growing a giant.

Since 1992, the world record has gone from 827 to 1061 pounds, and what was considered world class in 1992 (over 700 pounds) is considered rather normal for competitive pumpkin growers today. In 1994, four people broke the 900-pound barrier (Herman Bax, 990; Barry DeJong, 945.5; Glen Brown, 923 and Craig Weir 914) — that was a historic year. And since 1994, two have broken the 1000-pound barrier, and an additional ten people have cleared 900-pounds (two in 1995, three in 1996 and five in 1997). Even 900 pounds is becoming commonplace among the *Heavy Hitters.*

Certainly, Howard Dill remains the most important grower in the world based on his development of the *Dill's Atlantic Giant* pumpkin variety. No one has broken a world record using any other seed variety, and no one can compete fairly without using it.

Ray Waterman, another integral personality in the sport, still sounds the drumbeat as he continues to mesmerize the media and oversee the mecca of giant vegetable competitions in Collins, NY.

Above: Howard Dill in his patch in Windsor, Nova Scotia, Canada.

Howard Dill poses with his cat, Sneakers, and his 1996, 715-pound pumpkin. The Dill patch is the origin of the seed which all competitive giant pumpkin growers use today, Atlantic Giant.

I cannot fathom where the world of competitive pumpkin growing would be without the contributions of Howard Dill of Windsor, Nova Scotia, Canada. Almost single-handedly, he has refocused Canada and the world's interest in growing giant pumpkins. He was the first to break William Warnoch's 75-year-old world record and then proceeded to capture the world championship in four consecutive years beginning in 1978. With such success, Howard was inundated with requests for seeds that he had painstakingly developed through selective planting over a 30 year period. Howard later patented his variety in the United States under the name of the *Dill's Atlantic Giant* and the rest is history!

Every world champion pumpkin grown in the last 20 years has had its origins in Howard's pumpkin patch. If you are not using *Atlantic Giant ®* pumpkin seeds, you haven't a chance of competing. *Atlantic Giant* has been the great equalizer among men and women growing giant pumpkins. With it you can become a world champion, without it, the best you can do is perhaps 200 pounds.

Above: Howard with part of his extensive collection of hockey memorabilia.
Below: Howard Dill in his famous pumpkin patch in Windsor, Nova Scotia, Canada.

With further selective growing over the last twenty years, *Atlantic Giant* is now averaging 300-400 pounds, with many over 500 pounds, and in the hands of a competent grower, 800-1000 pounds has become a standard of excellence.

This could never have been achieved without the tedious, thirty years in which Howard planted in his patch, and his immense generosity in making this seed available to the masses. *Atlantic Giant*, which had its beginning in Howard's patch, created a renaissance of interest in growing pumpkins competitively. Without Howard Dill and the *Atlantic Giant,* there would be no sport of giant pumpkin growing as we know it today. There would be no 1000 pound pumpkins, no huge money prizes and no recognition for the average backyard gardener that plants *Atlantic Giant*.

This man is the Pumpkin King of our age. No one has garnered more recognition, more notoriety or more honors, via the pursuit of growing pumpkins, than Howard Dill. He is the stuff of which legends are made. In Canada, his name is as well known as the prime minister's. Amongst competitive pumpkin growers, he is a god. Without him, there would have been no need for a book on growing giants.

If that has not been enough for a lifetime of achieve-

ment, listen to what happened on the Dill farm, and tell me that Howard Dill has not lived a charmed existence. In the early 1800's men and boys on skates began slapping frozen cow flaps with wooden sticks on a slick frozen pond on the Dill farm, known as Long Pond. Many now consider the game played there as the origin of today's highly evolved sport of ice hockey, and Howard is considered to have one of the finest collections of hockey memorabilia in the entire world.

Howard's son Danny has inherited his love of growing pumpkins and collecting memories of ice hockey. Danny also runs the family business, which now sells more than the fruit and meat raised on the farm for five generations – he sells pumpkin seeds (some 5000-7000 orders per year), runs the seed museum and attends to a growing enterprise that supplies seed to seed distributors all over the world. Where Howard might have been awakened by the crow of a rooster, Danny's wakeup call comes from his fax machine as orders from Japan, England, Belgium, Italy, and elsewhere come in on a daily basis.

Howard Dill is still a farm boy, but he is also the Pumpkin King and a guardian of the exciting sport of ice hockey.

Top: The second, and present day Dill homestead built in 1878.
Above: The Dill's Atlantic Giant seed museum which has become a popular tourist attraction.
Left: Danny and Howard on Long Pond.

Ray Waterman is probably one of the most innovative and creative marketing men I have ever met. As co-founder of the WPC (the World Pumpkin Confederation) in 1983, he is profoundly responsible for the explosion in interest in the sport of giant pumpkin growing that has occurred over the last fifteen years. As director of the WPC, and coordinator of the Collins, NY weigh off, he has continuously sounded the drum beat for giant vegetables for many years — and when Ray speaks, people (especially the media) listen. He has garnered exposure for the sport in the *Wall Street Journal, USA Today* and the *New York Times*. He has appeared in a documentary film by the *Discovery Channel* and in October of any year, he is considered the leading authority on what is occurring in the world of giant vegetables.

An Olympics of Gardening

Visualizing Collins, NY as the mecca of giant vegetables, he dreamed of creating an Olympics of gardening that would show-off the best of what backyard gardeners can accomplish. Collins boasts competitions in pumpkins, squash, long

Above: Ray poses with one of his very best looking giant pumpkins in 1990.

gourds, watermelons, bushel gourds, cantaloupe, banana squash, asparagus-long bean, broad windsor bean, mammoth white radish, giant kohlrabi, onions, tall corn, sunflowers, tomatoes, long season beets, cabbage, long carrot, rutabaga and zeppelin cucumber, to name a few. Ray Waterman is the driving force behind the interest in competing and an excellent source of seeds for new and experienced growers through his seed company, P&P Seeds.

Ray is no slouch as a grower either. His heaviest pumpkin was grown in 1991 and weighed 780.5 pounds. He came very close to breaking 1000-pounds with a pumpkin in 1997. This pumpkin "went down" just a few days shy of the weigh off. Ray also holds the world record for long gourd at 99".

$10,000, $50,000 and $100,000 Prizes

The WPC paid Norm Gallagher $10,000 for a 612-pound pumpkin he grew in 1984 and threw in a trip to Hawaii for him and his wife, Ruth. When Ray saw the way new records were being established year after year, he was one of the first to predict a 1000 pound pumpkin before the year 2000, and he steadfastly implored all growers to join the quest in pursuit of growing the first half-ton vegetable.

In 1996, the WPC put up a $50,000 prize for the first to break the 1000 pound barrier, and that year, Paula and Nathan Zehr of Lowville, NY brought a 1061-pound pumpkin to Collins, NY, and went home $53,000 richer. In reaching ever further for new records, the WPC has offered a $100,000 prize for the first grower to grow a 1500-pound pumpkin (consult WPC rules). Who's to say that this prize won't be claimed in the next fifteen years. In the last thirteen years the world record has been bettered by 449 pounds. If we see the same increases over the next thirteen years, we'll be at 1510 pounds in the year 2010. We owe most of this enthusiasm for establishing new records to Ray Waterman.

A Consummate Marketing Man

Ray Waterman has been the P.T. Barnum of giant pumpkin growing for over fifteen years now. Nothing seems to slow his enthusiasm for the sport, and no one is more capable of attracting attention to the sport than he is. Constantly seeking new venues to promote the sport, and constantly in the forefront with new ideas, he has given the sport more exposure to average backyard gardeners than any man alive. From a handful of competitive giant pumpkin growers in the early 1970's, to thousands of serious growers in the 1990's, the sport has grown to enormous proportions. At last count, more than 2,000,000 people were growing *Atlantic Giant* pumpkin seeds world wide. This can only mean one thing — a lot of people have got the giant pumpkin growing bug! With so many people growing giant pump-

kins, and with so many competing, it just makes sense that the records will keep going up.

Maybe, a new world record will never be set, or maybe it will continue its torrid upward spiral — who knows? Maybe interest in growing giant pumpkins will wane in future years, or maybe it will be the number one gardening activity of the the new millennium — who knows?

But, from my vantage point, I can see no one more capable at promoting the sport to the world, or more effective at instilling a fierce competitive drive in backyard gardeners, than Ray Waterman.

Kelly Schultz, far left, owner of the Great Pumpkin Farm, along with Ray Waterman, third from the left, congratulates Paula and Nathan Zehr on their 1061-pound pumpkin of 1996.

Bill Greer grew a 1006-pound pumpkin in 1996, and along with a 1061-pound pumpkin grown by an upstate, New York couple, he was the first to break the 1000 pound barrier. This was a quest that began to take shape in the mid-1980's and became the obsession of every competitive pumpkin grower in the 1990's.

Like most world champions in the 1980's and 1990's, Bill came out of nowhere. In three short years he went from a novice, giant pumpkin grower to 1000 pounds. How did he do it? Well, growing pumpkins commercially didn't hurt him. Bill, who is now retired, farmed for many years growing crops like sugar pumpkins for the canning industry. This knowledge and experience gave him a keen edge in learning the science and art of growing giants. In three years his personal bests were: 150 pounds, then 373 pounds then 1006 pounds. In 1997 he had a 768-pound pumpkin, and three others that were over 700 pounds. He seems to have gotten off to a fairly good start.

Bill was born in 1932, has four children and eight grandchildren, and is now enthusiastically retired. He began growing giant pumpkins in 1994. That was a monumental year for giant pumpkin growers. That year, two Canadians and two Americans broke the 900-pound barrier for the first time. Herman Bax came as close as anyone had come to the 1000-pound quest when he weighed a 990-pound pumpkin at the Ottawa-St. Lawrence weigh off. Barry DeJong joined him at the same weigh off with a 945.5-pounder. I would suspect that it was pretty humbling to bring your first giant pumpkin to this same weigh off, and tip the scales at only 150 pounds. Thus was

Bill Greer removes the seeds from his 1996, 1006-pounder. Walls were a surprising 8 1/2" thick on one side and 11" on the other.

the beginning of Bill Greer's career as a competitive giant pumpkin grower. Two years later he would shock the sport of giant pumpkin growing with a 1000-pound pumpkin. The 1006 set a Canadian record that still stands at the printing of this book.

Fortunately, Bill knew from the very beginning that just average seed would never do if he was to improve. His insight and connections with top growers in the Ottawa-St. Lawrence Growers Association enabled him to secure and plant the best seed available in the world. The 1006 came from Tony Ciliberto's, 1994, 697-pound pumpkin. The genetic male-parent of the 1006 was Howard Dill's, 1994, 680-pound pumpkin. The 1006 was pollinated on July 1st, fifteen feet out on the main vine. Its final over-the-top measurements were 156" + 101" + 103" for a 360" total. Its estimated weight, using Bob Marcellus' tables, was 903 pounds. This pumpkin was more than 100 pounds over the estimate tables. Later, during seed recovery, wall thicknesses were measured at between 8 1/2" and 11". This was an unusually thick-walled pumpkin. In fact, as is the custom at most weigh offs, the largest pumpkin is weighed last. Upon visual inspection,

Above: Bill Greer talks with growers during a tour of his patch in 1997. Notice the fences and structures used for protection and the seed stocks planted (Holland's 739 on the right and Geerts' 946.5 on the left).

Bill's 1006 was weighed off fourth from last. This meant that there were three other pumpkins that appeared to be heavier than Bill's based on measurements and visual estimates. This is an example of how wall thickness can effect final weights.

This characteristic of good wall thickness made the 1006 a highly sought after seed stock. In 1997, its seed produced many large offspring including: Chris Andersen's, world champion, 977-pounder, Harold Baird's 854, Todd Kline's 787, and Ron Legras' 705.2. Bill believes that future world record pumpkins will come from a genetic background that has Tony Ciliberto's 697 in it because of its characteristic of good wall thickness.

Bill offers some sound advice to growers that stresses, "old fashioned farming practices." As I have often related to "wannabe" giant pumpkin growers, if you can grow tomatoes, you can grow giant pumpkins. As Bill relates, "Like pumpkins, tomatoes have to be started inside because of rela-

tively short growing seasons here in the North. The idea is to start your seed inside the greenhouse in late April, then when the plant reaches approximately 4" in height, transplant it outside into your cold frame.

"Plant the best seeds available, and get your soil tests done in the fall. Turn under lots of well rotted manure, or failing that, a crop of red clover ploughed-in is just as good. Your starter fertilizer should be 10-52-17 followed by Urea (48% N) to initiate plant growth, and later 20-20-20 for fruit growth. If you have it, use warm water, for watering."

Below: Bill at Ottawa weigh off in 1996 with the 1006, his wife Marguerite, daughter Janine, son-in-law Andre Audet and grandsons, Philip and Michael.

George Lloyd is another of the ever increasing number of growers to grow a 900-pound pumpkin. What distinguishes him is that he has done it twice, back-to-back — first in 1996 with a 909.5 (fifth in the world) and then again in 1997 with a 935 (second best in the world). In his first year of growing giant pumpkins, he grew a mere 687-pound pumpkin. He appears to be doing something correct. With his wife Deanna, in the last two years the top-thirty pumpkins have been peppered with the Lloyd name. Between the two of them they have grown a 935, 909.5, 880, 876.5, 874, and a 776. They have had more big ones in two years than most growers have in a lifetime. George also supplied plants to two other growers who grew world class specimens: Ken Armstrong with an 871-pound pumpkin (8th in the world in 1997) and first-time, 86-year-old grower, Harold Waterbury, with a 911-pound pumpkin that was weighed off at a small local competition. With numbers like these, George and Deanna would be good people to become friendly with.

Heavy pumpkins like these do not just happen; they require a lot of research, hard work and determination, but I found that George does not do anything unusual when growing his giants. In fact, most of his efforts are common sense, gardening basics. As he says, "I use lots of organic compost and manure (both horse and cow). I mix a good granular fertilizer into the soil before planting (one high in phosphorous and potash). From planting until blossoms appear, I use MiracleGro [15-30-15] then triple-20. Both are soluble and won't burn if applied on leaves.

"I use an insecticide / fungicide from the time seeds sprout until harvest. Both fertilizer and sprays are used every 7-10 days. I keep the patch free of weeds and grass. They rob plants of nutrients and give insects and disease a place to breed." All this sounds pretty basic! I guess the old saying, "Think big, but keep it simple," applies here.

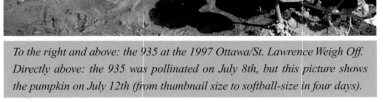

To the right and above: the 935 at the 1997 Ottawa/St. Lawrence Weigh Off. Directly above: the 935 was pollinated on July 8th, but this picture shows the pumpkin on July 12th (from thumbnail size to softball-size in four days).

o one epitomizes the sport more or illustrates the success that can come from growing the *Atlantic Giant* pumpkin seed better than Geneva Emmons. As a Washingtonian, she is blessed with not only geography but access to one of the very best pumpkin growers, and mentors, in the world, Joel Holland. A long time giant pumpkin grower, she never came close to growing a world class giant pumpkin until she was introduced in 1993 to the *Atlantic Giant* seed and in 1995 to a Holland 827 seedling. As she says, "For years, I have enjoyed growing *Big Max* pumpkins for my children (and the child in me)."

Her first attempt in 1993 resulted in a 387.5-pound squash. And as she remembers it, "I called Tallina George [the site coordinator for the Clackamas, OR giant pumpkin championship] for weigh off information and mentioned that my pumpkin had not turned yellow or orange yet.... Tallina remarked, 'My dear, you have a squash!' At that time I had no technical information about what was needed to grow a giant pumpkin, except to remove all but the one chosen fruit. Joel Holland recommended reading *How-to-Grow World Class Giant Pumpkins,* and sent me seeds.

My 1994 effort resulted in a 617-pound pumpkin. In May of 1995, Joel recalled that I had expressed an interest in growing a plant from the seed of his 1992, world record, 827 pumpkin, and asked me if I cared to have an extra plant that he had started. Needless to say, I accepted, and the forty-five minute trip to Puyallup brought an 827 plant in a four inch peat pot to Issaquah which resulted in my 939-pound pumpkin."

The 939 was the second largest pumpkin grown in the world in 1995, and ushered in an era for women growers — the top three pumpkins in the world in 1995 were all grown by women. The 939 was the 4th largest pumpkin ever grown in the world at the time.

What sets Geneva apart from average, competitive growers is her attention to giving the pumpkin plant the best microclimate that can be mustered. As she says, "It doesn't take a rocket scientist to grow one, but it sure helps to have a husband that is a retired rocket scientist." She credits her hus-

Below: Geneva poses with her 1995, 939-pound pumpkin just before severing it from the vine and crane-lifting it from the patch

band, Don, with much of her success as he eagerly helps to build greenhouses, the solar heated water system and installs pumps and plumbing where it is needed to water the plants. As you can see from the pictures below, this is no easy feat. The seedlings start in mini greenhouses that are tall enough to walk in, and are later replaced by 12' x 16' greenhouses made from plastic coverings and pipe. These large enclosures are designed so that the sides can be rolled-up on warm days. As Geneva says, "I felt that the covering would protect the plant from cooling rains that are so common in the Seattle area." As time proceeds, the plant's vines are allowed to grow under the plastic sidewalls and eventually the plastic is removed altogether. Later, shade structures are erected over the fruits. The photos below depict her methods, starting from top left and moving clockwise. In September, Don and Geneva construct a 4', clear plastic fence around the perimeter of their best plant, and drape floating row cover (Remay) over the plant and fence.

A complete measurement diary of the 939 is contained in *Chapter 13, Estimating Weight.*

len Brown is another repeater in the *Heavy Hitter* section from my first book on giant pumpkin growing, and he's earned it on the strength of his performance in a single season — 1994. In 1994, the world of competitive giant pumpkin growing was yearning for the first 1000-pound pumpkin, and although many were hoping that it would occur very soon, not many were showing real confidence that it could be done. No one had ever grown a 900-pound pumpkin and the record was 884 pounds. With the record being broken in consecutive years, 1992 and 1993, many were predicting a "down" year. What happened instead changed the attitudes of competitive pumpkin growers forever.

Glen had one of the most spectacular performances of all time when he recorded a new United States record of 923 pounds and grew another plant that had both an 867-pound pumpkin and a 790-pounder on it. From then on, people began to think seriously that the theory of one pumpkin per plant would have to be reevaluated. As such, the last three years have seen growers growing multiple fruit on plants and having extremely good success.

Glen is a strong advocate of crop rotation, and with the ample room that he has, he keeps vacant patches in rye and clover year round. He believes that seed selection is very important, and knowing the weather conditions for your area is crucial in determining whether you maximize the potential of your plants or not. He picks seeds based on their performance in past years, and he challenges the cool springs of Minnesota with greenhouse structures, and shade in the summer for the, almost, intolerable heat that they experience. To new growers he stresses that they plant only 2-3 plants the first few years so that they are not overwhelmed by the amount of work that it takes to properly care for them. If they can control weeds, water when needed, prune and bury when necessary, then they're ready for more plants. Most find 2-3 plants more than enough to handle.

Above: Glen's, 1994, 923. At the time this was the largest pumpkin ever grown in the U.S..
Below: 1994's 923, 876 and 790 — what a year!
Left: Glen with his 1994, 923.

923

867

790

here are few people who devote as much time to the sport and hobby of giant pumpkin growing as Al Eaton. Besides spending five, totally committed months growing his *Atlantic Giant* plants, the rest of the year he writes, calls and e-mails anyone he can find to compile data on over-700-pound pumpkins. He is one of the few sources who tries to include all of the top pumpkins in the world, regardless of where the pumpkin was weighed, and what world organization sponsored the weigh off. He has personally been the catalyst behind the idea of keeping and using family trees to aid growers in seed selection. See more in *Chapter 3, Family Trees.*

Al's growing career started in 1988 after seeing a friend garner much praise and recognition from the local media in 1987. He figured that if his friend could grow a 230-pound pumpkin, he could also. He was right, and for the last ten years, Al has been one of the top growers in the world. He was included in my first book, *How-to-Grow World Class Giant Pumpkins* as a *Heavy Hitter,* and along with Howard Dill, Ray Waterman, Joel

Holland and Glen Brown, he shares the distinction of repeating as a *Heavy Hitter* in the sequel. This was no easy task because since 1993 the ranks of competitive pumpkin growers has exploded and the availability of knowledge and access to good seed is much more widely distributed now.

When I asked Al what his most satisfying moment was, he responded, "Its difficult to pinpoint, but maybe the greatest thrill is doing your very best for five months, then going to a weigh off with an estimated weight in mind, only to find that your pumpkin weighs much heavier than the estimating tables. This is a real bonus. My 1996, 941 was 7% over the tables and my 1997, 853 was 9% over."

From the looks of it, no one will ever underestimate Al's expertise at growing world class giant pumpkins. Al's rules for cultural methods is summarized on the next page along with his career stats as a pumpkin grower.

Above: Al Eaton at the GPC, Ottawa / St. Lawrence weigh off with an 853-pound pumpkin. The 853 was 6th overall in Canada and 14th in the world in 1997.

Eaton's Career Stats

Year	Wgt.	Accomplishment
1988	259	1st, Ottawa Winter Fair
1989	278	6th, Canada; 5th, World
1990	581	
1991	348	1st, Canada
1992	661	5th, Canada; 16th, World
1993	721.5	Lost everything
1994		2nd, Eastern Ontario
1995	663	
1996	739, 805.5,	3rd, Canada; 4th, World
	941	6th, Canada; 14th, World
1997	853	

Eaton's Edict on Culture

- Prune vine growth heavily, limiting plant size to 800-1000 square feet. Bury all vines.
- Use styrofoam under fruit.
- Beware of stem stress.
- Use soaker hoses and avoid any stress from drought.
- Add some organic material every year.
- Do not use excessive amounts of chemical fertilizers.
- Monitor fruit growth carefully.
- Keep Cucumber Beetles under control.
- Reposition small fruit daily to create the best possible position of fruit to vine.
- Protect plant from frosts at both ends of the season.

Above: The 1996 Ottawa-St. Lawrence Growers Card Series.

Below: Al's patch demonstrates his desire to compete on a high level. His five plants have been responsible for some of the largest pumpkins ever grown in the world. My question is, "When do you fill-in the swimming pool?"

Although Craig Weir has been growing giant pumpkins since the late 1980's, I have known him personally as a friend only since 1994. I have great admiration for him, not only as a pumpkin grower, but as a good, honest and caring person. He is one of only two growers in New England to have ever broken the 900-pound barrier. His 914 in 1994 was 4th in the world and it sparked renewed commitment from New England growers in their quest to compete with the rest of North America. I saw the 914 in person and doubt that there has ever been a world class giant pumpkin grown that can compare with it, as measured by the qualities of shape, color and size.

At the time, I considered the 914 to be a fluke — a phenomenon that was not likely to be repeated in my lifetime. But, in the long run, it was but an early prophesy of what was to become common amongst world class giant pumpkins, and ushered-in an era of genuine confidence that the 1000-pound barrier would soon fall to someone.

Although Craig grows only one or two plants each year, he believes that this may be one of the reasons for his success. "It is better to concentrate your efforts on a single plant, than to plant many and not take good care of them." In 1994 when he grew his 914, it was his only plant, and since he strongly believes in a single fruit on a plant, it was his only pumpkin.

Since 1994, many growers have come to respect the abilities of Craig. He has uncanny intuition in regards to seed selection. His choice of growing the Holland 792 in 1994 began an era that saw

almost all competitive growers using that seed stock, and those of its parents (the Holland 827 and 722). Just as interesting was his decision in 1997 to use a seed from a lowly, 490-pounder that produced his most memorable pumpkin. Measuring a total of 385 1/4", it may very well have been the largest pumpkin ever grown. It fell to rot only one week before the world weigh offs. Based on estimates from the tables, it weighed almost 1100 pounds.

Above: "The one that got away," over 385 total inches and estimated at 1100 pounds.
Left: Craig Weir's 1994, 914-pound pumpkin.

Craig summarizes his process of selecting seed this way, "I only plant a seed that has a strong possibility of producing an orange-colored pumpkin with classic round shape. The pumpkin that the seed came from must be free of genetic problems, which will minimize the chance of their occurring in the offspring." He does a lot of research into seed stocks and does a lot of comparisons of estimated weights of pumpkins versus actual weights. Pumpkins that weigh far more than their estimates have genetic predisposition for thick walls, and thick-walled pumpkins are much preferred.

Craig believes that the most important element of growing a giant pumpkin is the quality of the soil. He tries to keep his soil as healthy and fertile as possible. He does this with lavish, annual applications of manure and seaweed, along with a cover crop of fall-sown winter rye. He firmly believes that one cannot maximize the growth of a seed and plant if his soil is not the best it can be. In season, Craig uses water soluble fertilizers at a rate that borders on insanity. He is quick to note that his sandy, loam soil may be able to tolerate the doses he applies, and does not recommend this practice to all growers. He mixes up to six different all-natural, plantfoods, including liquid seaweed and fish emulsion, in 55-gallon drums that he allows to warm and

To right: The vines are starting to really take-off. This signals the beginning of Craig Weir's intensive fertilizer program.

Below: Craig's daughter Kendall is credited with a significant contribution to the success in growing the 914. Here she stands inside it. This was one of only four, 900-pound pumpkins grown worldwide in 1994, and marked the first breaking of the 900 barrier.

stew for a week. He then uses a small submersible pump to apply the cocktail to the ground around each of his primary vines. He does this every week commencing with a plant size as seen above, and ending in mid-September. His use of 1/3 of a gallon of fish emulsion and one quart of liquid seaweed to each barrel results, over the season, in an application rate that is more than ten times the manufacturer's recommendations. From late July, liquid seaweed is discontinued as a soil drench, but applied as a foliar feed with a compression sprayer weekly to feed his plants and prevent powdery mildew.

His sandy, loam soil, combined with aggressive overhead watering, may leach away many of these plant nutrients, and the fact that he uses an all natural combination of plantfoods insures slower release and less likelihood of toxic buildup. He does daily overhead waterings (unless it rains) to insure even, moist conditions throughout the growing season, and believes that this results in less uneven growth and fewer problems with catastrophic failure of the pumpkin. He warns that this is not for every grower or every soil type.

He uses as little insecticide as possible but adds that failure to control the Squash Vine Borers will doom any effort you have of growing a giant pumpkin. He limits the use of insecticides, and instead, does close visual inspections of the plant on a daily basis to find and remove any borers that have entered the vine.

Few people have matched the success of Craig Weir growing so few plants. His 914 was a milestone for New England growers, and fueled the ever present debate amongst all world class giant pumpkin growers, "Who are the best growers in the world?"

Joel Holland ranks among the very best growers in the world based on his world record in 1992, with an 827-pound pumpkin, and his consistent, high level of performance all through the 1990's. Joel has grown many 700 and 800-pound pumpkins. He is one of a few repeaters as a *Heavy Hitter* from my first book on growing giants, *How-to-Grow World Class Giant Pumpkins*. He ranks as one of the most generous growers with respect to spreading the word on new cultural methods and giving away seed.

Above: Joel takes great care in transporting one of his giants. Here you see stems in water to keep evaporative water loss down, reflective foil on the rear and side windows to keep sun off the pumpkin and to keep the interior cooler and 1" styrofoam padding glued to the pallet to protect fruit from bumps in the road. This 740-pound pumpkin traveled 800 miles in 10 days and lost only 2 pounds.

He has pioneered ideas like proper seed stock selection, vine burying to promote root growth above and below leaf axils and heating water. Many western growers have taken his seeds and ideas and become highly successful themselves. They owe much of that success to Joel.

Joel is also an avid chronicler of his growing, and for several years has produced videos that explore growing techniques and top growers in Washington, Oregon and California. His videos sell for $25.00 and are well worth the cost. Price includes shipping and a free packet of seeds. Ordering information is available in the Appendix.

Along with his successful giant pumpkin growing wife, Mari Lou, their pumpkin growing has afforded them the opportunity to visit many places as guest-celebrities. In 1994 he was invited and attended the Japanese National Pumpkin Championship in Shodoshima, Japan and in 1995 and 1996 received all-expense paid trips to Disneyland where his pumpkins were carved and exhibited. In addition, as Joel writes, "Our great hobby of giant pumpkin growing has awarded us with a couple of other highlights we treasure. We spent time with Eddie Albert from 'Green Acres' and Hollywood fame, and had a chance to have coffee and visit with 'The Yankee Clipper,' Joe DiMaggio."

I would be remiss if I did not mention how important his two giant pumpkins grown in 1992 were to weight gains in the sport. That year his 827 was first in the world and his 722 was second. These two seed stocks produced scores of world class offspring in following years, and those offspring went on to produce still more. Along with Kirk Mombert's 567.5, I would consider the 827 and 722 to be the most productive producers of world class giant pumpkins of all time.

Joel Holland has elevated the sport of giant pumpkin growing from one of luck and good fortune to one of predictable results based on hard work, determination, skill and intelligent practices.

Constantly learning from others, constantly striving to be the very best, Joel Holland will be a top echelon grower for many years, and the people he mentors will be amongst the best tutored giant pumpkin growers on the face of the planet. His contribution to the sport will be hard to duplicate, and his goodness and generosity should be a role model for anyone growing giant pumpkins.

Top: Joel congratulates Pete Glasier at the 1994, Half Moon Bay weigh off where they tied with 696-pound pumpkins.
Above: Joel poses with his grandchildren, Jacob and Olivia, and the 1996, 807.
Right: Joel's wife, Mari Lou with the 1994, 700.5.

If ever there was a picture of perseverance and desire to succeed, it is James Kuhn. At 65 and retired from the United States Air Force, there seems little doubt in his commitment, and he has justly earned his rank among the best in the world at growing giant pumpkins. Although his hobbies include deer hunting and bee keeping (of which he presently has 50 colonies), his most rewarding pastime is giant pumpkin growing.

Jim has grown giant pumpkins since 1989, and through trial and error, has experienced continued success. Starting with a *Burpee's Prizewinner* in 1989, he quickly learned that to grow the real big ones he had to have better seed. Off to the WPC he went, and in 1992, armed with the *Dill's Atlantic Giant* pumpkin variety he grew a 447-pounder. In 1994 when the world saw four 900-pounders, Jim was plagued by a "root rot" that wiped him out. Discouraged but not ready to quit, he came back in 1995 with a 707.6-pound pumpkin and two others in the 500-650-pound range. That year he was disqualified from the Topsfield Fair All-New England weigh off for a small hole in the top of his pumpkin. Some think that this disqualification was unfair, but in any event, this would have caused many a pumpkin grower to quit the sport altogether. Down, but not out, James was once again wiped-out in 1996 from root diseases. But, 1997 would prove to be a year of atonement and long awaited recognition. He stunned New England growers with a 929.4-pound pumpkin which erased Craig Weir's New England record, and finally convinced me that 900 pounds was attainable by New England growers. In 1997, the 929.4 was 3rd in the world and James Kuhn missed the world championship by less than 50 pounds.

When I asked Jim what he felt was the secret to his success, he answered with much modesty, "As of this day, I cannot answer exactly what the secret is, or what the common factors may be. In my mind, there is no doubt that proven seed quality, aggressive pruning and burying of vines along with yearly additions of compost are essential. A weekly application of *Neptune's Harvest* fish emulsion was certainly a key ingredient.

"It is also very gratifying that in spite of the set backs, there was always support from fellow growers. I have to thank Tony Ciliberto of Wilkes-Barre, PA and Kirk Mombert of Harrisburg, OR for providing the best of seeds; and Don Langevin of Norton, MA and Al Berard of Sanford, ME for their encouragement and inspiration to continue after disappointments and let downs."

Above: James Kuhn with his 1997, All New England champion, 929.4-pound pumpkin. At 5' long, it left most of us in utter awe.

Behind this modesty is a fiercely competitive giant pumpkin grower... with a heart of pure gold.

T ony Ciliberto is a lifelong pumpkin grower who sentimentally recalls his grandmother's love of vegetable gardening (and particular, her love of growing pumpkins), and how that relationship instilled in him the desire to grow pumpkins and challenge himself to do it better each year. He remembers the day when his grandfather called him inside to watch a *Ripley Believe It Or Not* show which featured Howard Dill of Nova Scotia, Canada. He was totally amazed, and that amazement has since never abated.

He began to grow giant pumpkins in earnest in 1985. Up to that time, his best had been a 343-pounder. In 1991 he broke into the 500 club with a 502.5-pounder, and into the 700 pound arena in 1993 with a 734 (the world record that year was 884 pounds). In 1995, he grew his first 800-pounder with an 845, and he repeated the feat in 1996 with an 887 (his best to date). His 1994, 697 has Bill Greer's, 1996, 1006 as an offspring.

Few would question the commitment and sincerity of Tony Ciliberto. One of the most popular and loved of the top echelon pumpkin growers, Tony has served to introduce many to the sport and his friendship is valued by anyone who has had the privilege to meet or speak with him. At 43, this self employed masonry contractor and fine family man is a model for any aspiring world champion giant pumpkin grower.

Top: In 1993 with his 734-pounder.
Above: The 1996, 887-pounder.
Left: Trying to figure-out how to load the 734.

irk Mombert has been growing giant pumpkins for a long, long time. Since 1977 he has challenged himself every year to top his previous best, and in most cases, he has. From 348 pounds in 1983 (the world record was only 493.5 pounds at the time) to a career best 866-pounder in 1996, Kirk has steadily crept up the ladder of giant pumpkin growing success. But, all his success pales in comparison to a single contribution he has made to the sport.

The 567.5

In 1992, his largest pumpkin grown was a 567.5-pounder that was officially weighed at the WPC weigh off in Clackamas, OR. Joel Holland brought an 827-pounder to the Nut Tree, CA site and captured a new world record the same year, so the 567.5 was not an unusually large pumpkin for the times, but what has happened since has redefined what a hot seed stock is supposed to do. Kirk began to plant the 567.5 in 1993, and came away with a new personal best, 727 pounds. Still, very few growers took notice, and in 1994, Kirk grew another 567.5 and produced his first 800-

pound pumpkin, an 800.5. This captured the attention of many growers, and what has happened from 1995 until now is nothing short of amazing. In 1995, in the hands of top growers, the 567.5 produced five, 800-pound pumpkins (the largest being Jack LaRue's 875 and 850.5). Lyle Richert also had an 846.5-pounder, and Jerry Rose of Ohio had an 816. Kirk continued to better himself with an 833.5. In 1995, there were officially eight pumpkins grown from the 567.5 that were over 600-pounds, and several more in the 500's. Now, the word was out!

In 1996, the 567.5 was responsible for 18 of the top 50 pumpkins in the world (as recorded by Tony Ciliberto and Al Eaton), and it was clear to all that the road to successful giant pumpkin growing ran through Harrisburg, OR and Kirk Mombert. In tribute to Kirk, anyone who made a serious attempt at obtaining a 567.5 seed from him, got one. He gave nearly all of them away to fellow competitors. Many have used this seed to better their own personal bests. The biggest 567.5 offspring in 1996 was Jack LaRue's 897.5, while Kirk furthered his own personal best to 866 pounds.

Kirk Mombert at the Clackamas, OR, GPC weigh off with his 833.5-pounder in 1995. This is one of four pumpkins that Kirk has grown over 800 pounds.

By the winter of 1997, every competitive grower in North America was "chomping at the bit" to get a 567.5 for planting that spring. Those that were fortunate enough to plant one, again peppered the top 50 pumpkins worldwide. Ten pumpkins were recorded with weights over 723-pounds, with James Kuhn of Goffstown, NH stealing the honors of the largest 567.5 offspring with a 929.4. Jack LaRue also grew a 916.

I doubt that there will ever be another seed stock that will be so widely planted, and experience as much success as the 567.5. It will, undoubtedly, redefine the giant pumpkin as both beautiful and large, because most growers of 567.5s have grown bright, shiny orange fruit that have tender, fresh-appearing skin wrapped on deeply ribbed forms. The standard criticism of the *Atlantic Giant* is that

it is an awkward looking pumpkin. They're grown for weight, not looks; but the real bonus from the 567.5 is that most of the offspring have been fairly nice looking pumpkins. With so many of them planted now (approaching 500 worldwide) the offspring of this new generation of crosses may change the attitudes and perceptions of the average, giant pumpkin observer.

Kirk confessed to me, upon hearing of his selection as a *Heavy Hitter*, that one of his personal goals, after reading my first book, was to be in the next edition. He has earned this distinction by consistent performance and a long standing dedication to the sport. His 866 ranks among the largest pumpkins ever grown, and his gift of the 567.5 to other growers will continue to impact the sport for many years to come.

Above: Joel Holland films Kirk for his annual video on giant pumpkins.
Left: Kirk's 1997, 723-pounder which vividly shows the attributes for which the 567.5 has become famous: good color, fine, shiny skin and great shape.
Below: Kirk in his patch with his 1996, 866-pounder.

Whenever I hear the LaRue name, suddenly the 1960's song by Sly and the Family Stone, *It' a Family Affair,* begins playing in my head. Because, not only does the patriarch, Jack LaRue, grow world class giant pumpkins, but his wife Sherry and their daughter, Kayla, do as well.

Encouraged by Jack, a lifetime gardener, Sherry, a school teacher, took the sport up seriously in 1995 and grew a first-year 764. Her personal best is a 1016 that missed the 1997 GPC weigh off because of a minor blossom end split that occurred the day before the event. Her 764 in 1995, 676 in 1996 and 868 and 1016 in 1997 have to rank amongst the very best performances turned in by any giant pumpkin grower during their first three years of growing. Kayla, Jack's nine year old daughter in 1995, took a seed from a 1994, Nelson 910 (unofficial weight) and grew a 915-pounder. This weight was also unofficial because it was not weighed off at a competition, but it was hauled-off to a recycling center where an accurate weight was obtained 18 days after the pumpkin had been removed from the vine. A split in a rib at a scar, caused by Jack, lead to its demise. As he said later, "Kayla handled it better than I."

The LaRues are total gardeners.

They plant shrubs, trees, fruit, flowers and vegetables, and their relatively new homesite is continuously being recontoured to create plantable areas in the sloping landscape. From a small garden plot of 20' x 30' in 1990, their gardens now have increased to 10 plots measuring, in total, 130' x 178', and still the desire to expand continues. There are plans for sweet corn, *Burpee Prizewinner* pumpkins, giant squash and ordinary pumpkins.

This photo was taken at the LaRues' first competitive event in 1994. Jack and Kayla's 528.5-pound pumpkin finished tied for 17th.

Top of page: Avery LaRue, age one, inside a 443-pound pumpkin in 1996.

Kayla LaRue at age nine in 1995 with her unofficial, 915-pound pumpkin. The pumpkin was accurately weighed 18 days after being removed from the vine.

The LaRues may very well live in a gardening paradise, but don't suggest that to them because you may get some strong opposition. They have a long, cool and wet season that is in part the result of their proximity to the Pacific Ocean, and their geography, in a valley on the western slopes of the Cascade Mountains. They are only 20 miles southeast from the start of the southern rain forest of the Olympic Peninsula. There, annual rainfall exceeds 100 inches and all things grow to giant proportions.

Whatever the secret to the LaRues success is: weather, length of season or soil, they have been more successful than any other family in growing giant pumpkins in the 1990's. From 1992, armed with the *Atlantic Giant* and a new home in Tenino, WA, they have learned very quickly how to grow giant pumpkins and have moved even quicker up the ladder of top echelon growers. This has not been by accident as Jack and Sherry are both obsessive researchers and both have continuously modified their own growing techniques, and as a result, their techniques have evolved into a winning combination for them.

Always on the cutting edge, they were one of the first growers to use solar heated water, bury vines and use innovative pruning methods to manage the size and access to their plants. Their early season weather protection, watering systems and shade structures are thoughtful, as well as inspiring to any grower wishing to challenge himself to attain a new personal best. There has been very little luck involved with the success of the LaRues. Do the research, be creative and work, and you might also have the same success they have had.

A winter gale lashed seawater into 30' swells reducing old forest growth to driftwood. Note the size of these trees and tell me that this is not the land of giants.

Since 1992, their weights have been on an upward spiral, thanks in part to their relationship with other top growers like: Joel Holland, Kirk Mombert and Ron and Sharon Nelson.

Three 567.5's given to them in 1995 by Kirk Mombert were planted in

1995, 1996, and 1997. Jack produced an 875 and 850.5 on the same Mombert 567.5 plant in 1995, an 897.5 in 1996 and a 916 and 812 on the same plant in 1997. For three years in succession, Jack had grown a giant pumpkin over 850 pounds. He finished 4th overall in the world for three years running — that is world class giant pumpkin growing!

It has not been easy growing giant pumpkins in Tenino, WA. In spite of the beautiful pictures that appear here, much of the landscape has been altered to fit the needs of growing vegetables, fruit and trees. Hundreds of yards of topsoil were hauled in to create terraces on which to plant. Hundreds of feet of stone wall were constructed to hold the soil in place. If you've ever grown a world class giant pumpkin in earnest, you know how much work is involved in just caring for the plants. Imagine having to create the garden area in the first place before you can even consider the work of growing a giant. Most of us would have never started growing giant pumpkins. The desire is high and the level of commitment that the LaRue's exhibit is the key to their success. Forget about soil, weather, where you live or luck; if you have the desire and the commitment, you can be a world class giant pumpkin grower — look at a family that has proven this point. Where there is a will, there will be a way.

Above: A 1996 picture shows the LaRue cold frames. The large wooden structures support barrels, later in the season, which have cold well water pumped to them during the night. The water is allowed to warm during the day, and is then gravity fed to the plants in early evening.

Right: Sherry LaRue, with Jack on right, Gary Remlinger and the 1016 in 1997.

LaRue Family Pumpkins in the 1990's

Year	Pumpkin Weights
1992	141
1993	161
1994	528.5
1995	915, 875, 850.5, 764, and 560
1996	897.5, 680, 676, 671, 668.5 and 650
1997	1016, 916, 868, 819, 817, 812, 761 and 702

The LaRues compete at the All Northwest Championship, the GPC weigh off at Remlinger Farms in Carnation, WA, the Centralia Giant Vegetable Confederation and Half Moon Bay, CA. At each, they are top contenders among the likes of: Kirk Mombert, Joel Holland, Pete Glasier, Lyle Richert, Ron Nelson, Paul Handy, Don and Geneva Emmons, and collectively, some of the very best growers in the world. This is the "cream of the crop" of giant pumpkin growers, and among them, the LaRues have risen to the top.

Above: A picture showing the terraces that the LaRues have created to carry on their gardening pursuits.
Below: From left to right at the 1996, GPC, weigh off at Remlinger Farms: Kirk Mombert with his 2nd place 866, Jack LaRue with his 1st place 897.5 and Lyle Richert with his 3rd place 725.

robably no one deserves to be in this *Heavy Hitter* section more than Herman Bax. He did what we all dream about, and at the same time, what we all would consider to be our worst nightmare. Like running in an endless dream where we run as hard as we can, but can't quite reach safety, he came as close to growing the first 1000-pound pumpkin as any man can. In 1994, when four pumpkins broke the 900-pound barrier for the first time, Herman Bax's name was tops on the list of largest pumpkins grown in the world. The *Guinness Book of World Records* crowned him the undisputed world champion, pumpkin king and new world record holder. He missed certain immortality, and a legacy close to that of Roger Bannister's first, 4-minute mile. He missed 1000 pounds by 10 pounds with a 990-pound pumpkin.

To put this in perspective, a 990-pound pumpkin must gain, on average, eleven pounds a day for 90 days. From July 1st to October 1st is 92 days. In Canada, where Herman grows his pumpkins, the average pollination dates are from July 3rd to July 20th (so he had considerably less than 90 days to bulk up his prize winning 990). One more day, or perhaps as little as better weather on one day, and he would have been the first person to break 1000 pounds — I would still be running in my sleep!

The positive side of this achievement was, now everyone knew it was possible. It was just a matter of time, and they were all right; because just two years later in 1996, 1000 pounds was bettered by two growers (one in the U.S and one in Canada). Herman Bax had a lot to do with this achievement, because before you actually believe something can be done, it can't.

Herman Bax may very well be remembered as the man who came so close, but missed by the smallest of margins; but I will remember him as another committed, seriously competitive, giant pumpkin grower who showed the way to all of us who struggle with pumpkins half the size of his.

Left: Herman and Barry DeJong celebrate one of the most exciting achievements in the history of giant pumpkin growing — a one-two finish in the world. Here we see Herman's, 1994, 990.

Top of page: Herman, on left, is shown just moments from cutting Barry DeJong's 945.5 from the vine.

Middle of page: the 990 carved for display.

n 1994, I was mesmerized by Craig Weir's 914-pound pumpkin at the Topsfield Fair. I could not imagine anything, physically bigger. New Englanders waited for hours that day in anticipation of learning that it might be a new world record. But as we all know now, the 914 was but a member of an historic group of fruits that soundly broke the 900-pound barrier. Craig finished 4th in the world behind Glen Brown (923), Barry Dejong (945.5) and Herman Bax (990).

After the dust had finally settled, we were all looking for details about these pumpkins. Information like: pollination dates, distance out on the vine, number of segments, and the measurements, made for interesting reading. One of the bits of data that I was totally intrigued with was the physical measurements of Barry Dejong's 945.5. Mind you, I could not imagine anything bigger than Craig Weir's 914 which had a circumference of 160". When I saw the official, weigh off day data on the 945.5, I was stunned. Not only did it mimic the over-the-top measurements of the 914 (102" in both directions) but its circumference was a full 16" bigger at an incredible 176". Even the 990 (weighing in at 44.5-pounds heavier) had a smaller circumference of 162". Clearly, this fruit was huge!

Later, Barry DeJong published his diary which included notes on cultural practices, methods to initiate in 1995, and day-to-day data on all his pumpkins. After reading it several times, I came away with the feeling that Barry was a very unusual person in respect to his commitment to pumpkin growing. This was a serious, methodical practitioner with a sincere love of growing.

If you wish to follow in Barry's footsteps, compare your pumpkin's growth this year to the chart below.

Barry DeJong's Tale of the Tape

	OTT Measurements	Est. Wgt.
Aug. 2	190"	150
Aug. 4	212"	205
Aug. 19	303"	540
Aug. 20	314"	600
Aug. 23	321"	642
Aug. 26	334"	728
Sept. 1	351"	842
Sept. 4	356"	876
Sept. 7	362"	917
Sept. 10	365"	938
Sept. 13	370"	974
Sept. 15	376"	1018
Sept. 18	378"	1033

Oct. 1 Actual Weight	**945.5**

Right: Barry with his son, Scott, enjoying the site from atop the great pumpkin.
Left: Barry with his wife, Donna Marie and son, Steven with the 1994, 945.5.

hris Andersen came out of nowhere in 1997 proving again what I have preached since 1993. If you have good gardening skills and intuition, you can become a world champion giant pumpkin grower. In my first book I emphasized what Gordon Thomson (the first person to ever grow a pumpkin over 700 pounds – 755 in 1989) had told me was the secret of growing giants, "All you need is good seed, good soil, good weather and good luck!" All of these came into play for Chris in 1997.

Chris is one of the first to fully exploit the internet as a source of information for growing giant pumpkins. It is mind boggling that he came as far as he did in so short a time. His seed selections for the 1997 season were impeccable, showing a wisdom that sometimes escapes even the most veteran of growers. He aligned himself with veteran growers like Pete

Glasier and Rick "Doc Pumpkinstein" Dickow and became a good listener and fast learner.

He also had some good ideas of his own, and set out to achieve an 8%-10% organic level in his soil prior to the commencement of the season. His high California temperatures told him that cooling the plant on extremely hot days was crucial for him in maximizing the size of his fruit. He went about designing a cooling system that used micro-emitters that dispensed water conscientiously and effectively. By so doing, he experienced less leaf burn and wilt, and he kept the momentum of the plant's growth always moving in a positive direction. He also used an innovative technique to cool the micro-climate around newly opened female flowers to enhance the chances of good pollination. A picture on page 80 shows how he used bags of ice to create an ice house on the 100-degree day in which he hand pollinated his eventual 977-pound, world, champion pumpkin.

During the 1997 season, the 977 became known as "Jabba." Many growers name their pumpkins during the growing season, and this really demonstrates the bond they have with the fruit, and the commitment they have to seeing it achieve its maximum potential.

Left: Georgiana and Chris Andersen with their 1997, 977-pound, world champion, "Jabba."
Below: Chris with Pete Glasier and Rich Nolette on September 12th – three weeks before the world weigh offs. Notice the elevation of the vine.

And you thought that pumpkin growing was a man's sport — well look out! As we have learned in recent years, women are very good giant pumpkin growers. This was distinctly punctuated in 1995 when women grew the top three pumpkins in the world, and another four cracked the top twenty-five. Considering the fact that much fewer women compete than men, seven finishes in the top twenty-five shows a real skill for growing, not luck as some would have it.

I have known for years that women were better gardeners than men. I managed farm and garden centers for more than 20 years, and found that the lion-share of gardeners were women — and most of these women were accomplished gardeners. They were not just making the family purchases. They knew what they wanted and how to use it. Like most men, I have always seen pumpkin growing as a man's sport because men were the predominant competitors. At any weigh off, men will outnumber women by 5 to 1, but on average, women will outperform most of them.

Lorraine Orr, of the Ottawa-St. Lawrence Growers Association has done what all growers seek to achieve — grow big pumpkins consistently year-after-year. She has grown an 815.5 in 1995 and an 887, third in the world in 1996. In her first year of growing she grew a mere 600+ pound monster. There are very few growers in the world that have done as well over the last few years.

Right: Lorraine with her 5th in the world, 1994, 815.5.
Left: Lorraine with her 3rd in the world, 1995, 887.

To look at this shy, introspective registered nurse, you would be hard pressed to see anything that resembles the tough persona of the average male pumpkin grower. Speaking barely over a whisper, she commands the attention of some of the very best growers in an association that has been tops in the world in growing giants for several years.

If you doubt what I say, look at any organization of pumpkin growers and you will find women successfully competing against men. If you still doubt me, try averaging 851 pounds over your next two growing seasons, and I'll put you in the same class as Lorraine Orr.

ob Ruff was brought-up on a farm on the bluffs of the Mississippi River. He still lives there eight months of the year where he picks morels (edible fungi), digs ginseng (a close cousin of the Chinese perennial herb), traps, hunts and fishes. If you can't tell by now, Bob is an outdoor man. During the other four months he grows giant pumpkins and does a little farming.

Bob and his wife, Utoni, began growing giant pumpkins in 1989. I first heard of him in 1993 when he grew an 803-pounder. The world record had been set in 1992 by Joel Holland at 827 pounds. He was very close to breaking into a very select group of top echelon growers with a pumpkin that finished 8th in the world. But, his entry here in the *Heavy Hitters* is more for his model of consistency and high finishes all through the 1990's. His record of performance would be hard met by any grower anywhere in the world, and considering the enormous disadvantage that Iowa growers have with weather and "all the bugs that come from the cornfields," he has set a standard by which all mid westerners must measure themselves. Since 1993, he has grown a 700-pound pumpkin each and every year!

Bob knows that a 1000-pound pumpkin can be grown in Iowa if a grower can get a little luckier than he has been. He has been close on several occasions, but always lost them in the "homestretch."

Al Eaton said that his most enjoyable time spent with pumpkin growing has been his joy at seeing a pumpkin weigh much more than its estimated weight. Bob says that his most disappointing time was in 1995 (pre 1000-pound pumpkin time)

when he brought a pumpkin to the GPC weigh off in Anamosa, Iowa that measured-out at an estimated 965 pounds He was on the brink of doing something monumental and leaving his mark on the sport of giant pumpkin growing for all history to record. Instead, he settled for a 778-pounder and the 11th heaviest pumpkin in the world.

Bob advises that anyone seriously considering giant pumpkin growing as a competitive sport should choose their seed carefully. He looks for pumpkins that have both a tall shape (usually very large shouldered fruits) and weigh much more than their estimated weight. The thicker the pumpkin's walls, the more it will weigh over its estimated weight. Bob's most disappointing moment taught him the value of growing pumpkins with the genetic capability to have thicker walls.

The real sign of a successful person is the one who learns from his disappointments. Bob Ruff may have been disappointed in 1995, but it has not diminished his commitment to being the best pumpkin grower he can be.

Right: Bob with his wife, Utoni, with their 1992, 627-pound pumpkin weighed in Davenport, Iowa.

The Heavy Hitters

Canada

Herman Bax
RR#2
Lyn, Ontario
Canada K0E 1M0

Barry DeJong
RR#2
Brockville, Ontario
Canada K6V 5T2

Howard Dill
400 College Rd.
Windsor, Nova Scotia
Canada B0N 2T0

Al Eaton
Box 1217
Richmond, Ontario
Canada K0A 2Z0

Bill Greer
RR1
Picton, Ontario
Canada K0K 2T0

George and Deanna Lloyd
RR1
Simcoe, Ontario
Canada N3Y 4J9

Lorraine Orr
2352 Route 203
Howick, Quebec
Canada J0S 1G0

United States

Chris Andersen
8 Camelford Ct.
Moraga, CA 94556

Glen Brown
5702 229th Ave., NE
Bethel, MN 55005

Tony Ciliberto
1165 Pittston Blvd.
Wilkes Barre, PA 18702

Geneva and Don Emmons
4160 Peregrin Pt. Way, SE
Issaquah, WA 98029

Joel Holland
P.O. Box 969
Sumner, WA 98390

Jim Kuhn
116 Normand Rd.
Goffstown, NH 03045

Jack and Sherry LaRue
P.O. Box 1038
Tenino, WA 98589

Kirk Mombert
32415 Bush Gardens Dr.
Harrisburg, OR 97446

Bob and Utoni Ruff
20374 Imperial Ave.
Garnavillo, IA 52049-8042

Ray Waterman
14050 Gowanda State Rd.
Collins, NY 14034

Craig Weir
27 Ferry Rd.
Salisbury, MA 01952

Dill's "ATLANTIC GIANT"

Grown by:
HOWARD DILL
WINDSOR N.S.

chapter two

Seed and Sources

There are many authorized distributors of the patented Dill's Atlantic Giant Pumpkin variety, but most competitive growers acquire the seed they plant from fellow competitors.

If you want to grow the biggest pumpkin you can possibly grow, then you must use the *Dill's Atlantic Giant* pumpkin variety. In modern times, every world record has come from this variety. Since its introduction in the late 1970's, people using it have broken the world record ten times, and every world champion since 1979 has used this seed to grow their giant pumpkin.

Howard Dill, a Nova Scotia farmer, developed the variety over thirty years of trial and error experimentation with large varieties used by Canadian growers. Most notable was William Warnoch's world record 403-pounder (displayed at the 1903 St. Louis World's Fair). Its seed was distributed under the name of *Goderich Giant* for many years by the Rennie Seed Company in Ontario, Canada. The *Goderich Giant* was crossed with the *Genuine Mammoth* — another, popular, large variety that Howard's father had been growing for many years. The result was the *Dill's Atlantic Giant* which was patented in the United States in the early 1980's.

Howard Dill's grandson proudly poses in front of Howard's 1996, 715-pound pumpkin.

Almost every major seed company now carries the *Dill's Atlantic Giant*, and a list of them appears in the appendix of this book. However, when it comes to producing world class giant pumpkins, the source of seed, in most cases, does not come from distributors, but from the top growers themselves.

One of the most amazing things about giant pumpkin growers is their generosity in sharing information and seed. Since the average pumpkin can produce 500 seeds, most growers are willing to part with most of them, simply for the asking. Remember that most competitive growers grow less than four plants per year. The thought of grow-

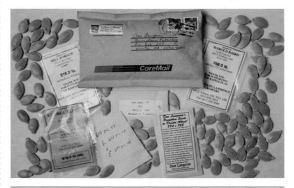

Above: Seeds shown here came from growers all over North America including the Ottawa-St. Lawrence Growers seed raffle and lottery and my own pumpkins.

ing all the seeds from even one of their pumpkins is not possible to begin with. Giving the seed away is the best way to find out how good they are.

From this sharing of seeds comes assurance that only the best seeds at producing large pumpkins will be planted each year — and this betters the chance of producing bigger pumpkins. If a grower is lucky enough to grow a pumpkin in which its seed continues over the following years to produce a high number of giant pumpkins, then that grower will be inundated by requests from competitive growers all over the world for his seed. This brings us to the interesting topic of seed stocks.

Seed Stocks

If you've ever been around pumpkin growers, you already know that their discussions revolve around three and four-digit numbers. These numbers refer to the weights of pumpkins, and the seed from these pumpkins is forever distinguished by the weight of their parent. Thus, when Joel Holland grew his world record 827-pounder in 1992, and in subsequent years it showed great promise in producing large pumpkins, this seed stock, the 827, became a very hot commodity amongst growers all over North America. Everyone wanted to grow one of these 827's, and along with Joel's 722 grown in the same year, these two seed stocks became the envy of every competitive grower. To show you how much of an impact just one pumpkins can make on the world of pumpkin growing, look at the list of offspring from the 827.

The 827

Joel Holland's, 1992 world champion 827 was one of the most prolific seed-stocks of all time. The notable 700 and above offspring from this pumpkin are too numerous to list here, but let me give you a few of the exceptional pumpkins that were grown from this seed. The following pumpkins were grown directly from the 827: the 93 Woodward 511(which had as its offspring, the 94 Bax 990, which had the 95 Orr 887, which had the

96 Eaton 941, and the 96 Kline 642 which had the 97 Schwartz 814); the 95 Fornof 816; the 93 Craven 836 (which had as its offspring the 95 Ruelle 839, the 94 Orr 815.5 and the 95 DeJong 945.5); the 95 Holland 800; the 93 Craven 755 (which had as its offspring the 94 Zehr 804, which had the 95 Zehr 963, which had the 96 Zehr 917, the 95 Marcellus 449 which had the 96 McIntyre 897, and the 95 Geerts 559 which had the 96 Geerts 946.5 which had the 97 Eaton 853, and the 96 Zehr 846); the 95 Emmons 939; the 93 Holland 782 (which had as its offspring the 95 LaRue 764.5 which had the 96 LaRue 676 which had the 97 LaRue 1016, the 96 LaRue 560 which had the 97 LaRue 817); the 94 Nelson 910 (which had as its offspring the 95 LaRue 915 which had the 96 Eaton 805.5); and the 94 Brown 923 (which had as its offspring the 95 McGinnis 398 which had the 96 McGinnis 810). Confused? I guess you should be, but in total, 27, 800-1016-pound pumpkins came either directly or from offspring of the 827. This is powerful proof that getting the right seed can lead to success. In a chart presented to me by Joel Holland, more than 75 pumpkins over 700 pounds can claim direct lineage to the 1992 Holland 827, and these are mostly officially weighed pumpkins. Many more pumpkins were grown over 700 pounds and never made it to a scale, or were never reported to Joel.

The 567.5

Kirk Mombert's 567.5-pound pumpkin, grown in 1992, after a slow reception from growers, gradually became the most sought after seed stock in the world by 1997. In 1996 and 1997, nearly a third of all the over-700-pound pumpkins in the world came from the 567.5. This white-seeded, seed stock has produced many world class giant pumpkins with most being fair skinned, shiny orange and deep ribbed. This seed stock, and its offspring, may redefine what future giant pumpkins should look like. See a further description of its offspring under Kirk Mombert in the *Heavy Hitter* section.

Plant What's Hot

Part of the excitement of growing giant pumpkins each year is knowing that you have seed that will make you competitive. This does not happen by accident. It requires research, networking and a commitment to growing. Acquisition of a hot seed stock will start with gathering information. This can be done by word of mouth, but reading the association newsletters will keep you abreast of what is most likely to produce the largest pumpkins next year (a list of associations appears in the appendix). The Ottawa-St. Lawrence Growers, with Gus and Joan Saunders, present an excellent breakdown of 700-plus-pound pumpkins each year provided by Tony Ciliberto of Wilkes-Barre, Pennsylvania. From this list you will find out who grew what during the past season, and what seed stock they used. From there, it is your own ingenuity that will determine if you will be able to plant the same seeds as the top echelon growers. You will have to communicate with the grower and develop a relationship — in short, you will have to make a new friend. Isn't this sport wonderful! In 99.9% of the time, a grower will freely give you seed and advice, so your odds of securing good seed are pretty good every year. You just have to know who it is that has the hot seed stocks. Of course, from time to time, you will run into growers that will not give you seed or any advice no matter how persistent you are. They have forgotten where they got their start, and have settled into a mood of, "I've got mine. Now you find yours somewhere else." Thank God that most growers are not like that.

Researching family trees can also reveal interesting traits that can lead to acquisition of seed with good potential. Some growers have great intuition for selecting what seed to plant by merely reviewing family trees and reading association newsletters. Some growers have used a method by which they measure a seed's worth by the amount of disparity between its estimated weight (determined by measurements) and its actual weight. They theorize that any pumpkin that weighs significantly over its estimated weight must have thick walls. Planting pumpkins with the potential for thick walls increases the chances that a pumpkin will weigh heavier than it looks. Remember, heaviest wins, not biggest.

I would be the first to remind you that getting that one, truly, mammoth giant pumpkin is a matter of luck. But, remember that the harder you work at finding a good seed candidate for your patch, the luckier you will get. You can average 500 pounds or more with most *Atlantic Giant* seeds, but if you're reading this book, who's looking for average?

Make as many friends as you can, because the road to success will most likely come from an unselfish pumpkin grower who likes you because you are interested in what he or she does. Start with the *Heavy Hitters* in this book or in my preceding book, or cruise the internet. There are a number of good internet sites and a message board where ample opportunity is available to anyone wishing to network with other pumpkin growers. A list of web sites and a message board appears in the appendix of this book.

Above: Tony Ciliberto's estimated 759 (a Mombert 567.5 offspring) went down from a split in a rib on August 23, 1996, but its seeds did well in 1997.

chapter three

Family Trees

Competitive pumpkin growers are rightfully obsessed with the origin of the seeds they plant each year. In recent years the idea of family trees for seed stocks has been given more and more attention.

Al Eaton has been growing world class giant pumpkins since 1988. And, in fact, he was featured in the *Heavy Hitters'* chapter of my first book on pumpkin growing. Al not only compiles the weights of many pumpkins grown in North America, he also researches, even further, into the pumpkins' backgrounds. He has preached to every grower who will listen, the concept of knowing the parents of every pumpkin they grow. He has compiled hundreds of family trees (four of which are presented in the following pages).

What is a family tree?

A family tree is nothing more than a genealogy report for a pumpkin's origin organized in a nice, easily-read, table. It tells you who a pumpkin's parents, grandparents and great-grandparents are (if data is available or known). Doing family trees for 30-50 of the largest pumpkins grown each year can reveal a variety of clues as to what seed stocks bear consideration for future planting. After all, seeds that show a high probability of producing large off-

Al Eaton of Richmond, Ontario, Canada stands before his 1996, 941-pound pumpkin. Al is credited with promoting the awareness of Family Trees and personally compiles much data annually. This chapter would not have been possible without him.

spring should always be preferred to those that do not have a clearly defined pattern of progeny.

The *Catch 22* is that seeds from the large pumpkin that you grew this season have not been tested and must be planted to prove their worth. You should not plant your unproven seeds, but on the other hand, every hot seed stock was at one time an unproven entity.

Family trees isolate interesting bits of information that may help you in choosing what seed to plant and what seed-stock to cross with it. Some growers have amazing intuition in choosing seeds for planting, while others grow what others have been successful with. Both methods work, but for every grower with uncanny intuition, there are hundreds that are successful by just doing what others have already done — plant what others are having success with. How do you determine this? You do it by reviewing as many family trees as you can each year to determine what truly has potential.

Give the seeds from your large pumpkin away to other growers, and evaluate how well they do with them before you commit a season. Since none of us is immortal, we only have so many years to grow giant pumpkins. Most of us can care for no more than four plants a year, so it seems sensible to plant wisely, and base our decisions on cold, hard facts — like those we get from family trees.

Four Family Trees

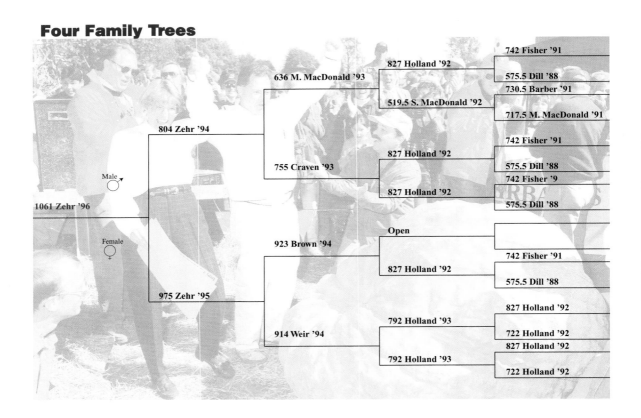

1061 Zehr '96

Male ♂

Female ♀

- 804 Zehr '94
  - 636 M. MacDonald '93
    - 827 Holland '92
      - 742 Fisher '91
      - 575.5 Dill '88
    - 519.5 S. MacDonald '92
      - 730.5 Barber '91
      - 717.5 M. MacDonald '91
  - 755 Craven '93
    - 827 Holland '92
      - 742 Fisher '91
      - 575.5 Dill '88
    - 827 Holland '92
      - 742 Fisher '9
      - 575.5 Dill '88
- 975 Zehr '95
  - 923 Brown '94
    - Open
    - 827 Holland '92
      - 742 Fisher '91
      - 575.5 Dill '88
  - 914 Weir '94
    - 792 Holland '93
      - 827 Holland '92
      - 722 Holland '92
    - 792 Holland '93
      - 827 Holland '92
      - 722 Holland '92

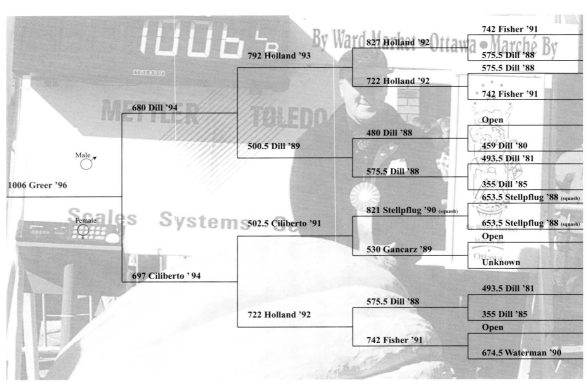

1006 Greer '96

Male ♂

Female ♀

- 680 Dill '94
  - 792 Holland '93
    - 827 Holland '92
      - 742 Fisher '91
      - 575.5 Dill '88
    - 722 Holland '92
      - 575.5 Dill '88
      - 742 Fisher '91
  - 500.5 Dill '89
    - 480 Dill '88
      - Open
      - 459 Dill '80
    - 575.5 Dill '88
      - 493.5 Dill '81
      - 355 Dill '85
- 697 Ciliberto '94
  - 502.5 Ciliberto '91
    - 821 Stellpflug '90 (squash)
      - 653.5 Stellpflug '88 (squash)
      - 653.5 Stellpflug '88 (squash)
    - 530 Gancarz '89
      - Open
      - Unknown
  - 722 Holland '92
    - 575.5 Dill '88
      - 493.5 Dill '81
      - 355 Dill '85
    - 742 Fisher '91
      - Open
      - 674.5 Waterman '90

990 Bax '94

Male

Female

721.5 Eaton '93

511 Woodward '93

827 Holland '92

718 Woodward '92

Open

827 Holland '92

742 Fisher '91

575.5 Dill '88

Open

717.5 MacDonald '91

742 Fisher '91

575.5 Dill '88

Open

674.5 Waterman '90

493.5 Dill '81

355 Dill '85

Open

600+ Dill '90

674.5 Waterman '90

Open

674.5 Waterman '90

493.5 Dill '81

355 Dill '85

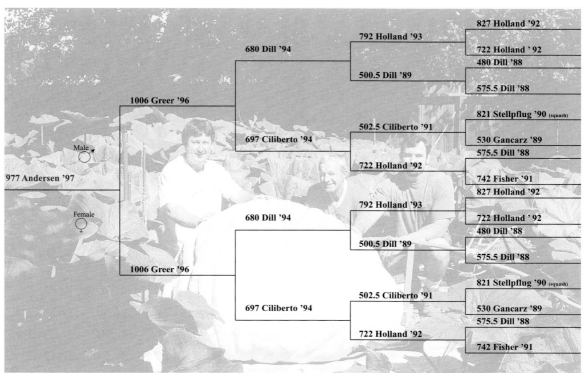

977 Andersen '97

Male

Female

1006 Greer '96

1006 Greer '96

680 Dill '94

697 Ciliberto '94

680 Dill '94

697 Ciliberto '94

792 Holland '93

500.5 Dill '89

502.5 Ciliberto '91

722 Holland '92

792 Holland '93

500.5 Dill '89

502.5 Ciliberto '91

722 Holland '92

827 Holland '92

722 Holland ' 92

480 Dill '88

575.5 Dill '88

821 Stellpflug '90 (squash)

530 Gancarz '89

575.5 Dill '88

742 Fisher '91

827 Holland '92

722 Holland ' 92

480 Dill '88

575.5 Dill '88

821 Stellpflug '90 (squash)

530 Gancarz '89

575.5 Dill '88

742 Fisher '91

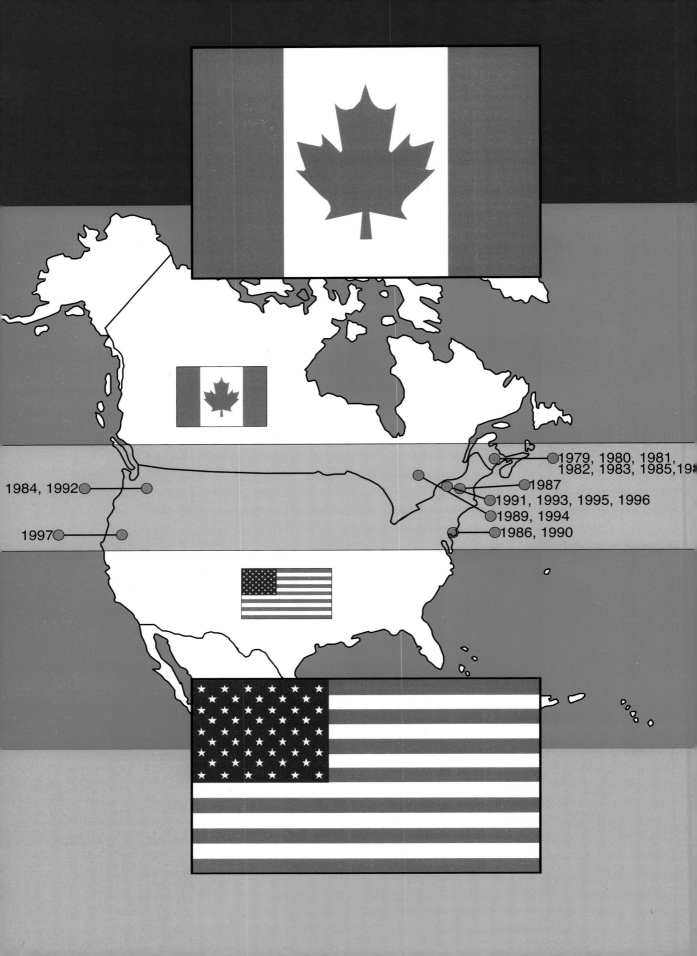

1979, 1980, 1981, 1982, 1983, 1985,19∗

1984, 1992

1987

1991, 1993, 1995, 1996

1989, 1994

1997

1986, 1990

chapter four

Sun and Soil

Selecting the site for your pumpkin patch is one of the most important decisions you will make; because without full sun and good, well-drained soil, you will be competing with a big disadvantage.

Assuming you have quality, *Atlantic Giant* pumpkin seeds, the most important decision you can make as a pumpkin grower is the location of your patch. I cannot stress enough the importance of sunlight. If your plants receive reduced sunlight due to trees, fences or structures, you will never maximize the potential of the seeds you plant. The amount of sunlight your plant receives will directly effect the size of the fruit it produces.

This statement has a great deal of historical backing. Take a look at where the world champions have come from over the last 19 years (let's call it the Orange Zone). All of these have come from a geographic band that stretches across the northern part of the United States and southern part of Canada. There are some surprising similarities in climate within this band, along with seasonal factors that make a strong point for where you live as being as important as what you plant.

The Orange Zone stretches across the North American continent from latitudes 40-46.

I have long thought that the length of sunlight days is a more critical factor in how big pumpkins get. After all, sunlight is the driving force of photosynthesis, and this is the process by which plants create and store energy. It seems logical to assume that the more sunlight your plant receives, the more energy will be created and stored.

One of the not so logical facts of nature is that the further north you go, in the northern hemisphere, the longer the sunlight days are in summer. This occurs because of the way light diffuses around spherical objects (the earth being a spherical object). The lower the sun is in the sky, the more diffusion occurs. This explains why Anchorage,

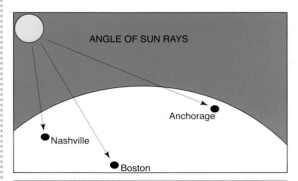

ANGLE OF SUN RAYS

Anchorage

Nashville

Boston

The angle of the sun's rays is more direct on Nashville than on Boston or Anchorage creating more heat, but shorter days.

Alaska experiences over nineteen hours of sunlight on June 21st (the longest sunlit day of the northern hemisphere). This sunlight is not as direct as it is further south, but it is longer in duration. The angle of the sun determines who is hot, and who is cold on earth. The lower angles of the sun associated with Canada and the northern US produce longer sunlit days but relatively lower temperatures. There is a great deal of agreement among competitive growers about a theory that says temperate summers are critical to maximizing pumpkin growth. Hot summers take their toll on plants by stressing their capacity to replace lost water and produce and store energy simultaneously. This is why you will never see a world record coming from Florida, or any area of the world where temperatures exceed 90 degrees often, and nighttime, cool-down, temperatures remain in the 70's.

As you travel north, you will experience longer sunlit days and, on average, lower daytime temperatures in summer. Sounds pretty good for growing giant pumpkins, doesn't it? The only constraint on how far north you can go is on the length of the frost-free season for that area. Remember that it still takes 120-150 days to grow a giant pumpkin from seed to harvest. As you go further north, this frost-free season becomes shorter and shorter, until time is not adequate to maximize the growth of an *Atlantic Giant* pumpkin. We are constrained in the south by diminished length of sunlit days and warmer temperatures, and in the north by a shortening in the length of the growing season and cooler temperatures. Somewhere in-between, an optimum geographic band stretches from east to west across North America where world records are more likely to occur.

These observations give strong reinforcement to the statement that the more sun your plant receives, the bigger the pumpkins will be.

I analyzed data supplied by the Astronomical Applications Department, U.S. Naval Observatory in Washington, DC for three cities in North America. They are Anchorage, Alaska; Boston,

Massachusetts; and Nashville, Tennessee. The next table summarizes data for the length of sunlight days on the 15th of the month for June, July, August and September 1997.

	June	July	August	September
Anchorage	19:01	18:25	15:48	12:54
Boston	15:16	14:58	13:53	12:30
Nashville	14:37	14:22	13:32	12:24

Notice that during the peak growing months, Anchorage would have 4 hours and 27 minutes more sunlight on July 15th, and 1:55 more on August 15th than Boston. Boston would have 36 minutes more sunlight on July 15th and 21 minutes more on August 15th than Nashville (see map above). This data confirms the fact that the further north you go, the longer the sunlight days in summer.

In summary, if you want to maximize your chances of growing your biggest pumpkin possible, plant it in full sun — or move to the Orange Zone.

Soil

Large pumpkins have been grown in all types of soil, from clay to sand, but in general, most large pumpkins come from soils that are well drained, high in organic content, and have a pH between 6 and 7 (6.5-6.8 is ideal). Sandy loams that have had a lot of manure and compost added to them have had the best results of all.

We do not always have the ability to choose what type of soil we will use, but we all have the ability to add and amend our soil to get the most from it. Manure, compost, mulches and cover crops can do a world of good for all soils along with fine tuning pH so that maximum uptake of plant nutrients is obtained.

pH

pH is the test by which you determine if your soil is optimum for the uptake of plant nutrients by your plants. pH is the measure of hydrogen ions in the soil, and is reported on a scale from 1-14. The higher the reading, the more alkaline (or sweet) the soil, and the lower the reading, the more acid (or sour) the soil.

Most plants thrive in an area on the scale around its neutral reading of 7. Plant growth can be fur-

ther enhanced by adapting soil to the best pH range for a given plant. It has been proven that pumpkins grow best on soils with pH between 6.5 and 6.8 (slightly acid).

You must first determine what your soil pH is. You can do this by testing with a kit purchased at your local garden center. Once you know your soil pH, you can adjust it by adding materials to the soil. This change will not happen quickly. It will take several months to adjust pH. If you have readings that are below 6, add limestone at the rate of 50 lbs. per 1000 square feet. Test again after 4-6 months to determine if further adjustments are needed. If your soil pH is above 7, then add sulphur, aluminum sulphate or ammonium sulphate (follow package instructions). pH can also be reduced by adding copious amounts of organic material. Decomposing materials always produce acid conditions which will reduce pH. Test again after 4-6 months to determine if further adjustments are needed. Getting soil pH into the ideal range will insure maximum uptake of major and minor plant nutrients.

The mother of all sources for organic material — the backyard compost pile.

Manure

The addition of manure and compost is integral to long term soil fertility. Competitive pumpkin growers have known this for many years. Manure and compost will not only add large amounts of slow release plant nutrients, but both add valuable organic material which aids in opening-up soil to air and water, and allows for good drainage while maintaining adequate levels of moisture.

Anywhere from 2-5 yards of manure can be added to each plant site. An average plant will cover 1000 square feet (approximately a 30' diameter circle). This manure should be spread evenly over the area, preferably in fall or very early spring — then tilled into the top 6" of soil.

Other Organic Materials

Seaweed is an excellent organic material source, as well as a supplier of major plant nutrients, trace elements and plant hormones. It has nearly mystical qualities that are just beginning to be exploited by competitive pumpkin growers. Craig Weir of

Salisbury, MA, who lives along the Atlantic Ocean, sings highly the praises of seaweed. After violent winter storms, his favorite variety of seaweed, Brown Rockweed, is dislodged from rocks and deposited on sandy beaches where it can be easily harvested. He washes it thoroughly to remove salt and then liberally applies it to his entire garden area. A 3"-4" layer of seaweed in the early spring spread over a fall sown crop of winter rye does nothing to discourage the rye. He then spreads additional manure on this and tills everything under. Craig believes in creating the best soil he can make, yet still uses water solubles, fish emulsion and liquid seaweed extracts throughout the growing season.

Above: A load of manure ready to be spread.
Below: On an ocean jetty in Salisbury, MA, Craig Weir collects Brown Rockweed Seaweed to apply to his garden in springtime.

Mulches

Mulches help to reduce the evaporation of water from soil, while they moderate soil temperature. They tend to maintain soils cooler during summer heat while they hold moisture that would generally be lost to sun and wind. Mulches can be almost anything organic including: grass clippings, straw, hay, salt marsh hay, etc. My favorite is compost made from the previous fall's fallen leaves, garden refuse and a liberal dose of fresh cow manure. From fall to spring, the pile will be reduced to a crumbly, blackish-brown soil additive that is unsurpassed as a building block of long term soil improvement.

I use it to hold down vines (with a scoop here and there) and as a mulch between vines to suppress weeds and slowly feed roots. Once the season is over, the compost is tilled-in to further improve the texture and quality of the soil.

Cover Crops

Cover crops in fall and early spring can be a valuable source of large amounts of organic material. Winter Rye is most often used in fall. It germinates and grows quickly. Sow at the rate of 20 lbs. per 1000 square feet as soon as refuse has been cleared from the patch in fall. Winter Rye will help prevent soil erosion in winter as it grows under the most extreme conditions.

In the spring, a foot or more of growth can be tilled-down, or you may mow it first and then till. This, so called "green manure," will open-up the toughest soils to air and water, and create ideal growing conditions for any plant.

Other green manures which can be used, depending on the time of year, are: annual ryegrass, red clover, green beans or peas. All of these can be sown on vacant portions of your garden during years in which no planting occurs. If you have the luxury of rotating your garden, don't forget green manures in the vacant, resting portions.

Above: A cover crop of Winter Rye sown in the fall germinates quickly to prevent winter soil erosion. The fast growing lush growth makes a perfect green manure to till-down in the spring.

chapter five

Seed Starting

Starting seeds can be easy if you know a few basics. If you've spent the time and energy to secure good seeds, and dreamt all winter about them, don't take anything for granted when you begin the season.

I f you read my first book, you know that I have an open mind concerning how giant pumpkin seeds should be started. Seeds can be started either indoors (indirect) or outdoors in the patch (direct). Both methods have produced world class giant pumpkins. In observing competitive growers the last few years, I would stress that most of them start seeds far ahead of the last frost date, and they do it indoors under controlled circumstances. Most use devices or procedures to elevate soil temperatures and some monitor soil temperature constantly to insure 80 to 90 degree heat. Under ideal conditions, pumpkin seeds should take 3-5 days to germinate. Anything longer than this means that seed vitality is not good, and prolonged exposure to moist, heated soil can lead to disease or death of the seedling. The key in starting giant pumpkin seeds is to get them up and growing as quickly as possible before seed leaves are exposed to overly long periods of moisture.

This seedling transplant is a fresh beginning to the new pumpkin growing year.

Preliminary to Planting

Germination times can be reduced by doing some preliminary work. Some growers will soak their seeds overnight in water or weak solutions of water soluble plantfoods or seaweed prior to the day of planting. Others will file the edges with a fingernail file to expose the interior of the seed to moisture. Both of these procedures introduces water into the seed case faster, allowing the seed root to emerge quicker and the seed case to unfurl easier once it is above the surface of the soil.

Above: Julie Langevin gently files the edges of a seed to expose the seed cavity to moisture.

You should use sterilized seed starting media to start seeds. You can find it at any garden supply center. Even if you are seeding directly outdoors, I encourage you to use sterilized media. Simply make a 1'x1'x1' hole and fill it with media. Plant your seed directly in this. When starting indoors, use peat pots which can be easily transplanted. Use the largest size you can find. Four inch diameter pots, or larger, are recommended. Remember that your seedling will outgrow its first pot in a matter of a few days, so the larger the better.

process not be delayed. Occasionally, a seed case will remain attached to the seed leaves, preventing this unfurling. At this time, a grower must gingerly remove the case by hand. This is a delicate operation that should not be undertaken casually. Once the seed leaves have completely opened, only then can a grower sigh a moment's relief. From here the seedling growth will be pronounced and rapid and preparations must be made for its transplanting outdoors.

Transplanting

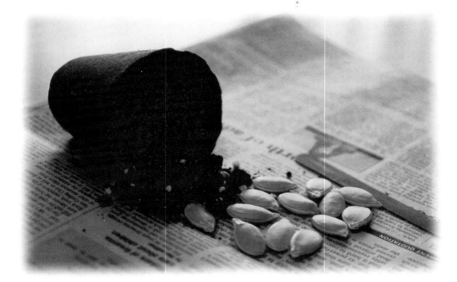

Most growers try to extend their growing season by planting ahead of the last frost date in their area. Pumpkin plants cannot tolerate frost, and seedlings are unbelievably fragile. Wind, cold weather and rough handling can all but eliminate any advantage you gain from starting early. If you are trying to get a jump on the season, I would still not plant any earlier than four weeks before your last expected frost. Most seedlings will be ready to transplant within two weeks of starting. If you start four weeks before your last frost date, you will still have two weeks of potentially damaging

When planting a giant pumpkin seed, the seed should be planted approximately one inch below the surface of the soil, and should be placed pointed side down. The seed root will come from the pointed end of the seed, and the energy stored in the seed will fuel the push of the seed case, containing the seed leaves, up through the surface of the soil.

Once the seed leaves are above the soil surface, they will unfurl to begin capturing sunlight to produce energy. Since there is only so much energy stored in a seed, it is critical that this unfurling

Above: Seeds, a file, a peat pot and some sterilized starting media — all you need to get started.
Right: A seed emerges from the media 3-5 days later.

frost. You must be able to further insulate or heat your outside structures to start this early.

A new seedling should be planted with great care in a protective structure, to shield it from damaging wind, cold days and frosty nights. The seedling can then be slowly acclimated to outside conditions by gradually introducing it to air movement during the day. This process is called "hardening-off" and will take anywhere from 1-2 weeks depending on weather conditions. Protective structures can be as elaborate as you want, or as simple as two storm windows nailed

together to produce a tepee over the seedling. The ends can be covered with plastic, and on exceptionally warm days, it can be tilted to one side to allow air ventilation, or completely removed if wind is not too severe.

The same procedures of seed starting should be followed for planting directly in your garden, but remember that soil temperatures can be very cold in spring — and cold moist soil can rot even the healthiest of seeds. Many growers will use soil heating cables in their hills to help elevate soil temperatures. This is particularly important for direct seeders, but I encourage all growers, either direct or indirect seeders, to use cables to help with early season soil temperatures. The combination of soil heating cables and protective enclosures above ground is a powerful combination for getting seedlings off to a fast start.

Above: Seedlings ready for transplanting.
Bottom: Howard Dill's pumpkin patch at planting time. Notice that apple blossoms coincide with the annual planting.

chapter six

Planting and Early Season Protection

Starting seed early does have its drawbacks. You will have to transplant the seedling into the garden soon after germination, and you will have to protect the tender plant from wind and cold weather.

I f you start your seeds four weeks before your last spring frost, and transplant as soon as the first true leaves begin to appear, you will have to protect your young seedling for two weeks against killing frosts. For the first 4-6 weeks outside, the seedling will have to be protected from the harmful effects of wind and cold weather.

Heating Cables

I have seen much achieved from the simple act of burying a heating cable, approximately 6 inches deep in an area of approximately 36 square feet (6' x 6'). Thermostatically controlled heating cables can be purchased at most garden centers. Although they are quite costly, $20-$30, they do give you a tremendous advantage when planting in early season, cold, ground. Used in conjunction with a mini-

greenhouse, they can give you a pronounced jump on the season. Placing them in the soil about one week before planting helps to warm and dry the soil prior to actually transplanting the seedling. Some growers will also cover the planting area with black plastic to heat-up the ground (black absorbs heat) and dry the planting area.

Above: Pete Glasier inspects his 3' deep planting location. This hole is refilled with rotted manure, compost and good soil to create the perfect starting environment for a new seedling.

Howard Dill's patch at planting time – the large, early season protection is essential in Windsor, Nova Scotia, where the season for growing pumpkins is brief.

Hills

The planting area is generally referred to by growers as the hill. The word hill goes way back in the history of gardening. Hill could refer to a raised area of soil, or to the act of planting more than one seed or seedling in a given area. As opposed to row planting where seeds are placed an equal distance apart in straight lines, hills are planted as groups of plants. When we refer to hills here, we are referring to a raised area of the ground. By creating a hill approximately 10' in diameter, with a central elevation that is at least 12" higher than the rest of the garden, and tapering the hill gradually outward, you create a raised portion of soil that will drain faster than the surrounding soil and heat quicker. This hill can be created simply by raking your garden soil towards the cen-

Above: This picture gives you an idea of plant spacing. Here, plants are spaced 25' apart, but if you have the space, 35' to 40' is recommended.
Below: One of Dave Stelts' good friends shows-off a mini greenhouse which housed Dave's, 1997, 801.5.

ter of the hill, or you can create the hill from entirely new soil using a combination of soil, aged manure, compost and other organic materials.

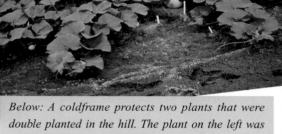

Spacing

Hills should be placed so as to give maximum space for the seedlings to grow. I would consider a 20' diameter growing area to be pretty much the minimum amount of space with 30'-40' recom-

Top left: A homemade mini greenhouse protects plants in early season. This design allows the plant a longer period of protective care.

Top right: Conservation fence makes a nice wind protective enclosure for plants up to 10' in length.

Left: Notice the slight mounding of the planting area which is indicative of the method of hill planting.

Below: A coldframe protects two plants that were double planted in the hill. The plant on the left was culled, the one on the right grew Craig Weir's 914.

65

mended. This means spacing plants between 20' and 40' apart. I emphasize the fact that the more space you give each plant, the bigger the plants and pumpkins, and the easier the care, in season. Spacing plants only 20' apart will require more pruning than spacing them 30'-40' apart. An average *Atlantic Giant* pumpkin plant can easily exceed 1000 square feet within the first twelve weeks of growth. Novice growers should not be discouraged if they have small planting areas. I have seen large pumpkins grown in areas that were under 500 square feet (20' x 25'), but plants grown in these small areas require more care, better vine management and luck. We will cover training, pruning and vine management later in this book.

Wind & Weather Protection

Nothing will benefit a grower more than protection of their plants from the wind and early season, cold weather. Small structures made from old storm windows can create greenhouse-like effects for young seedlings while they protect them from harsh winds. Placing a seedling out in the garden two weeks before the last spring frost is risky, so

protection must be planned for and used. A mini greenhouse, devised from whatever is at hand, can serve the seedling for 2-3 weeks. On nights when temperatures are expected to be below freezing, blankets and tarps can be placed over the greenhouses. If you decide to use heating cables along with your mini greenhouse, the extra heat they generate will practically eliminate the possibility of losing a seedling to frost.

Top: A walk-in structure sustains ideal growing conditions during the cool early season.
Bottom: Rows of corn form a wind barrier to protect the patch from buffeting winds.

Once the seedling begins to outgrow the mini greenhouse, there will still be need to protect it from the damaging effects of wind. I have used conservation fence with great results. This type of fence is generally used along wetland or conservation areas when new construction is taking place. It comes in 100' rolls with sturdy oak stakes stapled to it. By cutting a 100' roll into three pieces, you create a 33' fence, which when corralled, creates a circular enclosure of slightly more than 10' in diameter. This will protect your plant through the first 6-7 weeks of growth. Thereafter, as the plant begins to outgrow the area, it can be removed provided vines have begun to root to the ground. I have often repositioned the fence to get as much time out of it as possible. The tips of vines can even be trained under the fence to extend this period of protection.

The first eight weeks, from starting your seed to removing a 10' diameter wind enclosure, are the most critical in the life of your plant. If you are to grow a world class giant pumpkin, it will be because of what you do in these first eight weeks.

Above: A double enclosure of clear plastic protects the plant from buffeting winds that are prevalent in almost every full sun exposure.
Top left and right: This early season protective structure allows for up to 6 weeks of protection while creating elevated air and soil temperatures.

chapter seven

• Manure, Compost
& Granular Fertilizers
• Water Solubles • Watering
• Specialty Fertilizers
• Feeding Schedule

Feeding & Watering

If you've got good soil, you can grow a giant pumpkin. If you know how to feed and water, you could be a world champion. Maximize your pumpkin's true potential by feeding and watering when it's needed.

Giant pumpkin growers are obsessive feeders of their plants. In spite of glowing reports from their soil tests, they still add more organic, granular chemical and water soluble concoctions to their soil and plants. This behavior can be forgiven because the growing of giant pumpkins is not a commercial endeavor where expenses must be offset by income. It is a quest to be the best you can be, and in many instances, growers walk a thin line between maximum benefits from feeding, and injury associated with overfeeding.

Competitive pumpkin growers use the best from two opposing points of view on feeding plants. They use both organic and chemical sources for plant nutrients. They use organics for slow release, continuous feeding and chemicals for quick release where plant nutrient needs are high.

Craig Weir harvests seaweed from the shores of the Atlantic Ocean in Salisbury, MA. This is part of an annual ritual of collecting organic material to be used as soil additives.

Manure, Compost and Granular Fertilizers

In early spring, manure, compost and other organic materials can be added to the soil if it has not already been done the preceding fall. The addition of manure, especially fresh manure, should be done no later than four weeks before transplanting.

At time of planting, an application of a balanced, granular fertilizer insures that plant nutrients will be available in abundance. Formulations like 10-10-10, 10-6-4 and 5-10-10 can be applied at the rate of 5 pounds per 100 square feet. Higher concentrated formulations like 20-20-20, 15-15-15, 19-19-19 and others will require less. Read the labels for specific instructions.

Early Season Water Solubles

Upon transplanting, the use of water soluble plantfoods begins. The objective for early season is to provide plantfood for root growth so that plant roots can become fully established before the vegetative "rush" begins.

Root growth requires phosphorous. A water soluble plantfood with a ratio of two or more parts phosphorous to nitrogen and potassium is advised. Early season, cool soils retard the plant's ability to use phosphorous stored in the soil, even when abundant supplies are available. The use of a water soluble formulation fills a gap in the early season so that root growth is maximized. Commonly used water soluble formulations stressing phosphorous are: *MiracleGro* (15-30-15), *Agway Start 'N Gro* (16-32-16) and *EnP* (10-50-10). See the appendix for a list of plantfood manufacturers.

Early/Mid Season Water Solubles

As the soil gradually warms over the next 2-4 weeks, less emphasis will be placed on high phosphorous formulations, and more emphasis will be placed on high nitrogen mixes. Nitrogen is responsible for green growth — both leaf and vine growth. With an established root system, it is now time to see what your plant is made of. Nitrogen is highly water soluble and easily leaches from sandy soils (less so from heavy clay soils). The amount you use will depend on your soil type, and granular types may be substituted for water soluble because of their ease of solubility. The choice is yours. Some common products used are: Calcium Nitrate (16-0-0), Urea (48-0-0) or the common 10-6-4 which is used on millions of lawns in North America. However, the use of nitrogen has to be tempered. Green growth can come at the expense of blossom growth and fruit set as the plant roars through the patch. If growth is too fast, early fruit-sets may abort. You must walk the thin line between too much nitrogen (resulting in injury or fruit aborts) or not enough to maximize the potential of the plant.

The type of soil you have is critical in determining how much to use. Sandy loams will need more since they will leach it out quicker than heavy soils, but the best indicator of how much is needed can be determined from the color and condition of the leaves. You must never allow your leaves to reach a stage where they become bloated and dark blue-green in color. This is a sure sign that too much nitrogen is present. Leaves should be pale-green to grass-green in color. Leaves that are stunted or showing yellow margins will normally respond to additional applications of nitrogen plantfoods. Your leaves will "tell" you what the plant needs, if you are willing to "listen". The one way to become fairly adept at determining nitrogen needs is to visit as many patches as you can to compare the state of your plant to other top growers. Eventually, the perfect shade of green will form in your mind from which you will make comparisons and adjustments to your own feeding program.

A good, slow-release source of nitrogen is also present in fish emulsion. In the last 3-5 years, many world class growers have used it with amazing success. Since weights have skyrocketed in that time, I have no reason to doubt their judgement on its use. Fish emulsion is a fairly balanced product (2-4-0.5). It is great used as a foliar feed, once a week, throughout the growing season or as a drench on a weekly basis. Craig Weir mixes 1/3 of a gallon of fish emulsion to fifty-five gallons of water and applies it along the main and secondary vines of his plants every week from mid-June thru mid-September. Calcium Nitrate (16-0-0) and other formulations like *Peters Plantfood* (20-20-20) can also be used, or in combination with fish emulsion and other organic plantfoods. The key is to create a readily available, steady stream of

Above: Too much fertilizer creates dark, blue-green leaves that are bloated so severely that they collapse under their own weight.

nitrogen for your plant during this period. Vine growth may be as much as 2' per day, so abundant sources of nitrogen have to be available to maximize the growth of the plant.

Late/Mid Season Water Solubles

When female blossoms begin to appear, the push with nitrogen should be reduced. Some growers will rely on balanced water soluble formulations at this time like *Peters Plantfood* (20-20-20), *EnP* 19-19-19 with seaweed and other products.

If you become a keen observer of a pumpkin plant's growth, you will notice a few things over the years that are quite interesting — and which reinforce some of the cultural methods growers use to enhance the growth of their plants. I first became aware of these observations while growing other crops. For many years, I grew fall mums commercially. I also wrote a book on the subject, *The Growing and Marketing of Fall Mums,* which advised methods of pinching and feeding for timely growth. I did not invent these schedules, they all came from traditional methods employed by growers for many years. What I observed is that these schedules mimicked what occurred naturally. The grower either expedited what would have occurred naturally, or enhanced nature's response with his methods.

The same is true with growing giant pumpkin plants. Switching from one type of fertilizer to another is not what causes the changes in the stage of life of a plant. Rather, these changes in formulations enhance the stage of life that the plant has naturally assumed. In early season when plants are small, nitrogen is needed less; but as roots become established, the need for nitrogen increases as the vines begin to run. We do not cause this explosion of growth by our feeding methods — it occurs naturally. Growers try to enhance this growth by providing plant nutrients that are in need. The same is true when the time comes to reduce nitrogen. As the fruits begin to develop, vine growth

will begin to diminish. The rapid growth we observed in early/mid-season gradually slows as the plant begins to store energy in the fruit, rather than use it for development of leaves and vines. This is why termination (pruning) of the primary vine (covered in *Chapter 10, Training and Pruning*) may not be necessary. Even the main vine will slow to a standstill as a large pumpkin gains weight. Reducing nitrogen at this stage makes sense because less green, vegetative growth is occurring. We do not cause the reduction in growth by using less nitrogen, the plant just slows down and we accommodate its new needs for a more balanced formulation of plant nutrients.

Feeding methods employed by competitive giant pumpkin growers have evolved to mimic what occurs naturally — and to maximize these natural stages of development. They do not cause them. This is an important point, because it once again emphasizes observing your plants. Watch for the changes in your plant's stage of life which trigger new needs and new plantfood formulations to meet these needs. Watch your plant's leaves and vines for signs that a new growth stage has begun, or is about to begin. In early season, a small plant's growth is slow and its needs are for phosphorous for root growth; in early/mid-season, the need is for nitrogen as vines begin to run; and in late/mid-season, more balanced formulations of plantfood are needed to supply the vines, leaves and also the newly developing fruit. Finally, it is time to maximize the size of your pumpkin, and for the remainder of the season, the emphasis will be on potassium.

Late Season Water Solubles

Late season growth is characterized by a slowing of vine and fruit growth. In New England this occurs around mid-August or about six weeks after pollination (approximately 15-16 weeks after transplanting). The vines and leaves are still growing, but not at the amazing rates that occurred 4-6 weeks earlier. The pumpkin's rate of growth has slowed and sustaining that slow growth, along with safeguarding the fruit's health, through the remainder of the season is the primary goal of a competitive giant pumpkin grower. The next 4-6 weeks can be an agonizing time if you have an extremely large pumpkin that you plan to compete with at a weigh off in early October. Will it make it to the weigh off? Will it gain another 50, 100 or 200 pounds?

Above: Neptune's Harvest liquid seaweed plantfood has gained much popularity among competitive growers in recent years.

Keeping your fruit supplied with the plant nutrients it needs to sustain its growth is emphasized, and fruit growth requires potassium. So, as the vines have begun to slow, less nitrogen is needed, and more potassium is required to keep the momentum of fruit growth continuing. Formulations like *Peters Plantfood* 15-11-29, Potassium Nitrate (14-0-46) and others are recommended. Notice that we still continue to feed nitrogen, but the emphasis has clearly shifted to potassium. Potassium is responsible for carbohydrate development and pumpkins are carbohydrate storage areas for the plant. Leaves, through photosynthesis, take the sun's energy and produce sugars which at this time of the year are not used for development of more leaves, but stored in the fruit as excess manufactured carbohydrates. Keeping

the plant working, without over stressing, becomes a delicate balance that only careful observance of leaves can maintain.

Specialty Fertilizers

We touched briefly on the use of fish emulsion earlier, but its use, along with other specialty plantfoods, cannot be overstated. As growing methods for giant pumpkins have evolved over the years, the use of fish emulsion has become more prevalent in the arsenal of amendments used by giant pumpkin growers. It can be used both as a foliar feed for leaves or as a drench for roots. Both methods have widespread use among growers. Its slow release provides nitrogen and other major and minor plant nutrients at a rate that maximizes uptake without the serious side effects associated with chemical fertilizers.

Another commonly accepted plantfood is seaweed. Seaweed extracts and fish emulsion both contain many trace and minor elements, and plant scientists are just beginning to understand their impact on plants from an amino acid, enzyme and hormonal perspective. Seaweed has been shown to contain three valuable plant hormones that will enhance growth of all plants. *Auxins,* when present in stems, will enhance cell elongation (enlargement of cells) and when present in roots, will inhibit growth of the plant to promote more aggressive root growth. This statement taken literally might serve to recommend seaweed as a drench in early season to promote root growth, and as a foliar spray after to promote elongation of cells. *Auxins* also help to improve pollination by reducing aborts. *Cytokinins* promote the growth of secondary vines, acting opposite to *Auxins* which promote or discourage the growth of the main vine. *Cytokinins* also enhance bud and flower formation. *Giberellins,* which are also present, help with germination by starting enzyme production that helps in the nourishment of the plant embryo. These three hormones, although not entirely understood, create conditions that seem to favor optimum growth for pumpkins.

You can purchase seaweed in liquid form as an extract or as a powder that can be reconstituted and then sprayed. There are many good manufacturers of seaweed products. My favorites are Neptune's Harvest, and Age Old Organic/EnP. See the appendix for other plantfood manufacturers.

Seaweed has seen a dramatic increase in use by competitive giant pumpkin growers over the last five years. Considering the increase in the average weight of giant pumpkins over that time, I see no reason to discount its effect. I have used it for the past two years, and have grown a personal best each year. I think that its use will lead to less catastrophic losses like stem stress or other season-ending failures. Research has shown that it can also dramatically reduce late season attacks of powdery mildew when applied to the leaves on a weekly basis. The condition of my pumpkins at weigh off time were far superior to anything I had previously grown — and these pumpkins held-up longer after harvest. These observations have not been proven by all, but I have seen enough to whole-heartedly endorse the use of seaweed products.

Watering

Water is what makes it all happen. Water brings dissolved plant nutrients, both major and minor, to the producing areas of the plant. Water from soil fills the ever increasing need for replacement caused from evaporation and transpiration. 80% of the weight of a pumpkin is water. Water is stored in every cell, in every part of the plant. The importance of water, and its continuous and consistent supply, should be the focus of any aspiring giant pumpkin grower. Pumpkins need huge amounts that are in part determined by weather conditions, soil type and the size of the plant. Water can also be used as part of a cooling microclimate strategy where misters are regularly turned on to wet leaves during periods of severe heat. This cooling effect, called evaporative cooling, has been used effectively by many competitive pumpkin growers who live in parts of the world where summertime heat is not temperate. Chris Andersen used it in

sunny California in 1997, and against all odds, grew the largest pumpkin in the world that year (977 pounds).

How much water is needed is a difficult question to answer. Soil levels should be kept moderately moist at all times. This can be aided by applying mulches to the ground around and between the growing vines. Salt marsh hay, straw, compost and very old and aged manure may be used. The goal is to insulate the ground with a layer of material that retards evaporation and promotes cooler soil. On average, a plant will need a minimum of 1" of water per week, but most giant pumpkin growers rely on much higher levels. Observing soil conditions and leaves is the key to determining whether adequate moisture is available, and can be utilized quick enough to replace that which is lost during the conditions of the day. Sometimes, no amount of water will satisfy the needs of the plant, and flagging of leaves will occur. Flagging indicates heat stress, and if you experience much of this, and soil moisture levels are high, you should consider some way of cooling the plant's micro-climate. Turning-on an overhead sprinkler for 20-30 minutes may be your answer. Windy conditions can also accelerate the loss of water, so wind screens could benefit those who garden in areas that are both hot and windy.

Water can be applied overhead through sprinklers or beneath the leaves with drip hoses, or both. The use of drip hoses has become quite popular in recent years because of the desire to keep water from dissolving pesticides that are present on the leaves. Overhead sprinkling will require more pesticide spraying, unless of course, you are using a systemic insecticide and fungicide program.

Watering should be consistent as well because most of the catastrophic failures of pumpkins like: stem splits, Dill rings and blowouts (covered in *Chapter 14, Murphy's Law*) are compounded by soil levels that oscillate from very dry to very moist over short periods of time. The rapid growth associated with adding water to parched soil, which an aggressive plant has claimed, can lead to an enormous explosion of growth. This explosion of growth will generally do damage to the fruit by causing any weak conditions to be stressed even more. As my good friend Hugh Wiberg once told me, "Slow and easy wins the race." Watering should be moderate but consistent so that the level of moisture in the soil stays fairly constant. This can be accomplished by more frequent, shorter interval, watering and by mulching the ground, in and around the plant.

Above: Chris Andersen's innovative misting system allowed a southern California grower, growing under high heat conditions, to become world champion. Chris', 1997, 977 was heaviest in the world.

Below: Kirk Mombert's elaborate watering system allowed him to become one of the best growers in the world over the last five years.

Feeding Schedule

	Plantfood	Application
Week 1*	xx-**XX**-xx / Seaweed	Soil drench†
Week 2	xx-**XX**-xx / Seaweed	Soil drench
Week 3	xx-**XX**-xx / Seaweed	Soil drench
Week 4	xx-**XX**-xx / Seaweed	Soil drench
Week 5	**XX**-xx-xx and Fish / Seaweed	Drench-broadcast / foliar spray≈
Week 6	**XX**-xx-xx and Fish / Seaweed	Drench-broadcast / foliar spray
Week 7	**XX**-xx-xx and Fish / Seaweed	Drench-broadcast / foliar spray
Week 8	**XX**-xx-xx and Fish / Seaweed	Drench-broadcast / foliar spray
Week 9	**xx-xx-xx** and Fish / Seaweed	Drench-broadcast / foliar spray¥
Week 10	**xx-xx-xx** and Fish / Seaweed	Drench-broadcast / foliar spray
Week 11	**xx-xx-xx** and Fish / Seaweed	Drench-broadcast / foliar spray
Week 12	**xx-xx-xx** and Fish / Seaweed	Drench-broadcast / foliar spray
Week 13	**xx-xx-xx** and Fish / Seaweed	Drench-broadcast / foliar spray
Week 14	**xx-xx-xx** and Fish / Seaweed	Drench-broadcast / foliar spray
Week 15	**xx-xx-xx** and Fish / Seaweed	Drench-broadcast / foliar spray
Week 16	xx-xx-**XX** and Fish / Seaweed	Drench-broadcast / foliar spray△
Week 17	xx-xx-**XX** and Fish / Seaweed	Drench-broadcast / foliar spray
Week 18	xx-xx-**XX** and Fish / Seaweed	Drench-broadcast / foliar spray
Week 19	xx-xx-**XX** and Fish / Seaweed	Drench-broadcast / foliar spray
Week 20-22	Seaweed only	Foliar Spray

* -Week 1 in New England would be approximately May 1-8 (about two weeks before the last frost).

† -Soil drench is done by completely dissolving plantfood in water and applying from the base of the plant and extending 3' out. As plant grows, a larger area will be fed and more plantfood will be used. High phosphorous (P) plantfoods (xx-**XX**-xx) like *EnP* (10-50-10) and *MiracleGro* (15-30-15) along with liquid seaweed should be used.

≈ -Drench-broadcast / foliar spray - This week marks a shift from high (P) plantfoods to high nitrogen (N) formulations (**XX**-xx-xx). Granular, high, (N) fertilizers can be applied to the ground at a rate of a half pound per 100 sq. ft. or water solubles used as a drench according to package instructions. Calcium Nitrate (16-0-0), and Urea are good choices. Granules should be applied just before anticipated rainfall or watered-in after broadcasting. Again, apply from the base of the plant and extend 3' out. Use liquid fish emulsion as a drench and begin using liquid seaweed as <u>both</u> a foliar spray and as a drench.

¥ -This week marks the transition from high N to balanced formulations (xx-xx-xx). We still continue to use fish emulsion as a drench and seaweed as <u>both</u> a foliar spray and as a drench. Balanced plantfoods could include granular 10-10-10, 19-19-19, 17-17-17 and others and water solubles like *Peters Plantfood* (20-20-20). Broadcast granules at the rate of one half pound per 100 sq. ft. and apply water solubles as a drench.

△ -This week we begin the last push to harvest. Balanced formulations are now replaced with high potassium plantfoods (K) (xx-xx-**XX**). Muriate of Potash (0-0-60), Potassium Nitrate (14-0-46) and *Peters Plantfood* (15-11-29) are good choices. Broadcast granules at the rate of one half pound per 100 sq. ft. and apply water solubles as a drench. Use fish emulsion as a drench and seaweed as <u>both</u> a foliar spray and as a drench.

• Cross- and Self-Pollination
• Male and Female Flowers
• Pollinating Techniques
• Avoiding Aborts

chapter eight

Pollination

*Hand-pollination serves two worthwhile purposes.
It allows for pollination under extreme conditions
as early as possible, and it allows for
selective breeding of desirable traits.*

Pollination is the act of delivering male pollen to the female flower parts, and successful pollination results in what growers call "fruit-sets." You know a pumpkin is set if it continues to grow and shows no signs of slowing or discoloration. If a female flower is not successfully pollinated, it will abort, wither and die from the vine. This process may be very quick, or it may take upwards of two weeks. Experienced growers can tell within 48 hours whether a pollination is successful. Fruit in the process of aborting will gradually lose that brilliant, shiny, fresh appearance, and gradually adopt a pale, dull color.

Pollination can be accomplished in many ways. It can be done by bees as they collect nectar from the flowers. This is referred to as open-pollination where the exact source of male pollen is not known. Pollination can also be performed by hand, by man. Hand-pollination can be either self-pollination or cross-pollination. When the male pollen comes from flowers on the same plant as the

A newly set fruit marks the beginning of the most exciting time of the growing season. The flower will soon wither and dry, but the shiny yellow fruit will begin growing at an unbelievable rate.

female, this is referred to as self-pollination. If the pollen comes from male flowers on plants other than the plant the female flower is on, this is called cross-pollination.

The purpose of hand-pollination is twofold. First, intuitive crosses can be made by selectively pollinating one plant with another. The result of these crosses will be demonstrated by the seed offspring in future years — pollination does not effect the genetics of the plant you are growing, only the seed inside the pumpkin it is growing. Second, and more important, hand-pollination assures that pollen will be delivered to the right place at the right time under all circumstances. Nature, by way of bees and other insects, does a marvelous job already, but a grower's intervention allows for earlier and more selective pollination. It is this early intervention that is most important because the longer the fruit is on the vine, the longer it can potentially grow.

Cross-Pollination

Cross-pollination relies on the use of male flowers from one plant and female flowers form another. A grower will do this to create seed offspring that have a better chance of demonstrating a desirable trait that is present in one of the parents. Usually the goal is just increased weight, but by analyzing what contributes to weight in a pumpkin, a grower might introduce characteristics like: thicker walls, taller shapes, bigger ribs, etc.. They may also try to introduce genes from pumpkins that have experienced less catastrophic failure like: stem splitting, blossom end rot or Dill rings (we'll cover all of these later). Growers will also cross-pollinate to try to create giant pumpkins that have better shapes and better color – but I think this kind of cross-pollinating does not occur very often among top echelon growers. As is often said, "Giant pumpkin competitions are not beauty contests." The bigger your pumpkin is, the bigger your successes will be in the sport of pumpkin growing.

Some growers have amazing intuition when it comes to cross-pollination. It is important to note that most crosses made are between the heaviest pumpkins that can be found, or they are between pumpkins that have shown a high probability of producing large offspring. In either case, breeding large with large has probably been the reason why weights have soared over the last ten years. Selective cross-pollination between big pumpkins assures, over the long term, that offspring will also be large. Any seed stock that consistently produces 600-pound pumpkins can, potentially, produce a world record pumpkin – and the world of pumpkin growing will flock to the door of a pumpkin grower who has this seed stock. The world, via the pumpkin "grapevine" is very, very small. So, it is survival of the fittest, or might I add, survival of the heaviest.

Self-Pollination

Self-pollination is the use of male flowers from the same plant as the female flower. If you plant only one plant, you have no alternatives to self-pollination. Sometimes, though, self-pollination is intended for the same reasons as cross-pollination — perhaps to assure that positive characteristics continue. But, in most cases it is because male flowers from other more desirable plants are not available.

Remember that hand-pollinating techniques are almost always done for the sole purpose of enhancing the probability of a successful fruit-set. Getting a pumpkin set early should be a primary goal of all competitive growers.

Male Flowers

Pumpkins are by far one of the easiest plants to pollinate. Where most plants have microscopic pollen grains, pumpkins have huge particles that can be seen with the naked eye and felt between the fingers. These yellow, dusty granules can be collected from the male flowers and then deposited on the female flower parts with a small artist's brush, or the male flower can be cut from the vine and taken directly to the female flower. It is advised that you strip the petals off the male flower, being careful not to knock the pollen off of the anther, before you begin applying it to the female flower. Use the stem of the male flower much the same way as the handle of a artist's brush as you delicately touch the pollen-loaded anther to the female stigmas.

Male flowers are characterized by their long, thin stems which sprout from the vine at the leaf axils. They usually precede the appearance of female blossoms (which occur at the ends of the vine) by 5-7 days.

Above: Howard Dill displays the "artist's brush" method of hand pollinating. Notice that the petals have been stripped from the male flower.

Above: The end of a vine shows a female bud along with all of the plant parts for the next leaf and axil. Below: A female flower ready for pollination.

Female Flowers

Female flowers appear only at the ends of vines and their flower buds are attached to a small pumpkin. An early detection would find these small pumpkins to be no bigger than the size of a small pea. Each of these small pumpkins is attached to the vine with a short stem.

The vine growth pushes on, leaving the female blossom protruding from a leaf axil. The blossom will open about 7-10 days after its first appear-

ance. At that time, and for only the first 4-6 hours that it is in bloom, it is ripe for pollination.

Female flowers contain internal flower parts that are called stigmas, but are referred to by pumpkin growers as either segments or lobes. Each segment has a thin tube, called a style, that leads down into the pumpkin to an ovary. It is through this tube that a single, germinated pollen grain will pass to fertilize the seeds within that ovary. Since each pollen grain has its own unique genetic blueprint, each ovary that is successfully fertilized will be unique. If you have five segments then you have five tubes and five separate ovaries. A female flower will usually have four or five segments with six and seven-segment flowers appearing far less frequently.

Some growers have raised important questions about the genetic uniqueness of seeds in each ovary, and have begun to harvest seeds in a more organized manner. Harvesting seed by ovary allows growers the opportunity to evaluate the performance of a single ovary and to make better judgements about the likelihood of a particular type of offspring. This method is still in its infancy, being pioneered by Ron and Dick Wallace and John Castellucci of Rhode Island, and still remains a significant question to answer. If proven, this method should allow growers to more accurately predict their seeds' offspring.

Pollinating Techniques

Since the window for a good pollination is so small, just hours after the blooming of flowers, planning a hand-pollination is important. Only freshly opened flowers can be used.

Many growers will mark the location of flowers the day before they are expected to bloom. With experience, this becomes a fairly easy task. These candidates for pollination are then covered with cheesecloth, paper bags or small, plastic, vented vegetable storage bags. I have found that these work best because of their zip-lock closures that fit securely around the blossom and stem. This is done to completely isolate the flower parts from any intrusion by insects. Bees, foraging for nectar, can bring with them pollen grains from other plants. If you want to be absolutely sure about the origin of pollen grains, then isolation of both the female and male blossoms must occur. Covering them the night before they open protects them from early morning invasions prior to hand-pollinating.

The primary reason for hand-pollinating is to insure early fruit-sets. Isolation is not necessary if you are not concerned about who the genetic parents are. Growers still mark flowers the night before, but they may leave them fully exposed to bees, before and after hand-pollination, to insure maximum probability of successful pollination.

Hand-pollinating should start as soon as there are female flowers available and continue until mid-July. A zone of time which lasts from late June through mid July has been the most productive time for producing world class giant pumpkins. I

discontinue hand-pollinating after July 20th because the time for growing a large pumpkin is diminishing. After this, I pinch-off female buds to give maximum benefit to fruits that are already set. During the hand-pollination period, I do not withhold pollination to any female flowers. I mark each with date, genetic male pollinator and number of segments. Later I will evaluate this data in conjunction with measurements of growth and shape and position on the vine to determine whether to cull or keep a particular pumpkin. This will be covered in more detail in *Chapter 9, Fruit Selection.*

Avoiding Aborts

Many times, your best efforts at hand-pollinating will result in fruit aborts. This is particularly discouraging if you are aiming for the "golden time-zone" between July 1-10. Factors within your control and factors out of your control will affect the likelihood of a successful pollination. The conditions of the plant and weather will mightily affect pollination outcomes.

Chris Andersen's ice method for cooling the micro-climate around a newly opened female flower increases the probability of a successful pollination on hot days.

Plants that are aggressively producing leaves and vines are strong candidates for aborts. These plants are still in their vegetative growth period, perhaps prolonged by more than adequate amounts of nitrogen plantfood availability. Slowing the plant's vegetative growth is not easy, but supplying less nitrogen at this time may produce a plant reaction that helps the transition into a more balanced growth period. That is why we suspend high nitrogen fertilizers just before the "golden time-zone" to enhance conditions for slowdown. See the *Feeding Schedule* at the end of *Chapter 7, Feeding and Watering.*

Weather plays an important role in successful pollination. If it is too cold or cloudy, flowers will be slow to open and bee activity will be reduced. More so, if it is too hot, aborts are highly likely. Too hot can be defined as temperatures above 90 degrees. A few growers have actually tried to cool the micro-environment by placing bags of ice around the female blossom. This technique was first brought to my attention by Barry DeJong (of 945.5 and *Heavy Hitter* fame). Pete Glasier, Chris Andersen and Ron Wallace have all used this technique with success. First, you cover the blossom with a large styrofoam container to insulate and moderate the temperature. Then you create a tent over the styrofoam container with a white

plastic trash bag. You place a 20-pound bag of ice around the tent, and replenish the ice a few hours later. This method is extreme, but it works. If you miss the "golden time-zone", you will probably not have as big a pumpkin this year as you could have had.

Ice is extreme, so shading the female flower, and light, overhead watering to create evaporative cooling, are techniques that can be employed before resorting to the extreme.

A cross section of a female (left) and a male flower (right) shows distinctly different flower parts.

chapter nine

Fruit Selection

Selecting an early fruit to grow-out to maturity is a "crap shoot." There are no tried and true methods for determining which fruit will grow the biggest. With that said, here are a few rules that competitive growers use.

Years ago, the commonly accepted rule on growing giant pumpkins was that there should be only one pumpkin on a plant. This rule has been challenged many times over the last few years, and gradually, growers are coming to the realization that the *Atlantic Giant* pumpkin plant has "energy to burn." Some growers have even questioned the need to cull-out pumpkins at all, while others have modified the way in which they select pumpkins for final growing-out. Most now believe, and I am in agreement with them, that the *Atlantic Giant* can sustain and achieve maximum potential of multiple fruit on a plant. I have seen situations where four and five fruit were left to mature, and each reached respectable size. John Castellucci of Smithfield, RI grew a plant in 1997 from his 682.4-pound pumpkin of 1996 in which four pumpkins were allowed to grow. Each attained a weight of over 600 pounds with one official entry weighed-in at 733 pounds. He had close to 2800 pounds of pumpkin on a single plant. Of course, the skeptic would say, "What would his weights

have been if he had culled to one or two fruit?" I say, probably the same. There has been ever increasing confirmation that a fruit receives its energy from only the primary vine it is on. Other primary vines do not effect its growth, and the inference is that you can have multiple fruit on a plant as long as they are on separate primary vines. If you have three primary vines (the main vine plus two other strong vines emerging within 18" of the base of the plant) then you can potentially grow three pumpkins on the plant.

Which of these pumpkins you choose for the final push can be helped by applying some common sense, intuition and evaluation of the fruit based on: rate of growth, shape, vine location and position and the number of segments.

Rate of Growth

If you measure the circumference of each of your pumpkins beginning at a size that is slightly larger than a basketball, you will accumulate data, over time, that will effectively tell you which fruit is growing the fastest on the plant or vine. You must take into consideration the time of pollination of each, because the earlier pollinated pumpkins will be larger. You will be able to determine at a very early time, which is growing the fastest. In the early part of the season, you will be collecting

Sherry LaRue's 1997, 1016 was sculptured and then named the Queen of Sheba. Having the ability to choose a candidate like this one, early in the season, to grow to full maturity takes experience, skill and luck.

data only. No culling should be done until fruit reach at least 50 pounds and you have had sufficient time to evaluate all of the pumpkins on a plant or vine. Having 8-10 pumpkins on a plant in mid-July will in no way affect the final weight of your largest pumpkin. In fact, some believe that having more fruit on the vines at this time, in which vegetative growth is still particularly strong, acts as a moderating force on reducing fruit aborts or splitting from excessive, quick growth. If you've grown giants before, you probably have experienced a pumpkin that splits in two overnight, as if someone had hit it with a hatchet. With more fruit on the vines commanding needs, I think less of this splitting should occur, especially with multiple fruit on a vine early in the season.

Cull gradually through the season, first eliminating slow growers and then evaluating other factors.

Fruit Position

The position of the fruit, in relation to the vine, is an important consideration when making a determination if a fruit should be culled or be left to continue to grow. All fruit will need some adjustment early in their life to achieve their best position relative to the vine (we cover this in *Chapter 10 - Training, Pruning and Fruit-Protection)*. Some will have better positions than others. Also, short-stemmed pumpkins may have later problems that can occur when the shoulders of the pumpkin enlarge to such size that they begin to touch the vine and push it until the vine tightens forcing enormous pressure on the stem. Having a fruit on the outside of a curving vine is better than having one on the inside of a curving vine. Vines that curve away from the fruit are less likely to experience stem stress.

It is interesting to note that the shape of these large-shouldered pumpkins, although they present problems related to stem stress, are the preferred shape for heavy-weighted pumpkins.

Segments

As we touched on earlier in *Chapter 8, Pollination,* segments are female flower parts which tell us how many ovaries a particular fruit will contain. The basic premise is that the more ovaries (and subsequently more seeds) you have, the bigger the pumpkin will become. In my first book, I presented an argument that may have discouraged growers from considering 4-segment fruit if 5- and 6-segment fruit were available. In the past couple of years I have noted the appearance of many 4-segment fruit in the top pumpkins grown annually; and therefore, I cannot discourage anyone from choosing one if his instincts tells him that this is the best pumpkin they have. Looking at the data for 700+ pound pumpkins for 1996 and 1997, I found that out of 122 pumpkins, 64% were 5-segment fruit and 24% were 4-segment. This does not prove that 4- and 5-segment fruit are preferred, but suggests that they are more

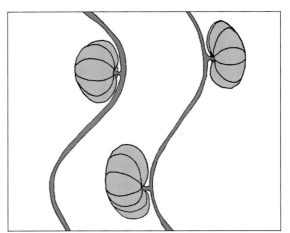

Right: The vine on the left has a fruit set on the inside of a curve which can present problems later in the season. The vine pattern on the right is much preferred over the length of the growing season.

likely to occur in 700+ pound pumpkins. I would still tend to want to keep a 6-segment fruit over a 5-segment one (or a 5-segment over a 4), but its emphasis in the decision making process should be treated with less significance based on what has occurred the last two years.

Shape

I have seen heavy pumpkins that were tall and beautiful, and I have seen heavy pumpkins that were flat and ugly, so including a section on shape has me wondering whether it will do more to confuse a new grower than to instruct. Nevertheless, there are some shape preferences that can help in determining which fruit you will cull and which you will grow-out if you have two on the same primary vine. Tall pumpkins are much preferred to short pumpkins if their total measurements (circumference combined with over-the-top measurements) are equal. In fact, many growers have observed that estimates of weight derived from the tables can be skewed in either direction simply by the height of the pumpkin. Pumpkins that have heights (ground to the highest level that the pumpkin stands) below 30" will weigh less than the tables, pumpkins that have heights between 30" and 36" will be very close to table estimates and pumpkins with heights above 36" will weigh heavier than the tables. This generality is not true in all instances, but with most pumpkins it will help a grower in deciding between two pumpkins that have similar total measurements but differ in shape and height.

Skin Type

Another rule that has garnered much acceptance in the past five years involves skin type, and how it effects the divergence of a pumpkin's actual weight from an estimated one derived from the tables. If two pumpkins measure exactly the same, then the one with the ruddier complexion will weigh more. Pumpkins with shiny, soft skin will weigh less than pumpkins with rough hardened exteriors. Many times, the roughened specimens will exhibit skin patterns that resemble the netting on cantaloupes. "Cantalouping" seems to indicate that actual weight will exceed estimates. These are only general rules and actually, the condition of skin may be more indicative of the stage of life the fruit has entered. The longer the fruit is on the vine, the harder the skin appearance will be. Skin appearance may very well indicate the stage of maturity that a pumpkin has attained — and since most growers believe that end-of-season weight gains are more the result of wall thickening than actual increases in measurements of the exterior, hardened-skin pumpkins may just be pumpkins that have attained a higher level of maturity than their fair-skinned competitors. These fair-skinned rivals may have had several more weeks of growth left in them.

Primary or Secondary Vine

The goal should be to set a fruit on a primary vine. Many times you will pollinate and set fruit on secondary vines and the question begins to emerge about which place is ideal for maximum pumpkin growth. In 1996 and 1997, of all of the Great Pumpkin Commonwealth's 700-pound and over pumpkins, only 9% were on secondary vines. 91% of the world's largest pumpkins in 1996 and 1997 were grown on a primary vine. This is strong statistical evidence that you have a much better chance of growing a world class giant pumpkin on a primary vine. At times, you may not have this luxury, but if you do, and you have a choice between two pumpkins, fairly equal in all respects, then the primary vine pumpkin is the better of the two. If the secondary vine pumpkin is on a vine that comes off of the primary vine which contains your other candidate, then the secondary vine pumpkin should be culled from the plant.

As you can see, you will use many different variables to determine final fruit selection, and all of these can improve your chances of selecting the best fruit to grow-out. Along with evaluating the rate of growth, shape, vine position, skin type and number of segments, your own intuition will have to be used as well. This may be the most important part of the analysis, for in the end, you must make the decision. As probability and chance have it, you may make a wrong decision, or you may make the right one.

chapter ten

Training, Pruning
& Fruit-Protection

*Nothing is questioned as much, or more
misunderstood, than pruning a giant pumpkin plant.
Plant management boils down to mimicking nature
and using some common sense.*

robably the most asked question by a
novice giant pumpkin grower is, "When
and what do I prune on my plants?"
This is never an easy question because
there are so many methods used by good,
experienced growers, and picking what is best,
sometimes becomes quite difficult.

Good growers with experience prune based on the
needs of their individual plants. Aggressive plants
are pruned differently than slow growers, and
plants with more than one, fast-growing fruit are
pruned differently than plants with solitary fruit.

In general, a basic set of rules does exist, from
which departure is made occasionally to enhance
or retard the growth of the fruit.

*Aggressive vines appear to be growing as you watch
them. Day-to-day growth can sometimes be as much as
2' on a robust primary vine.*

Primary, Secondary and Tertiary Vines

We all start with a main vine from which, close to
the main root, other almost equally aggressive
vines can develop. A plant will generally have 2 to
3 very aggressive vines that emerge in this first 18
inches of growth. Trained properly from the start,
these 3 to 4 vines form the main skeleton of the
plant, and early management of these vines
ensures maximum use of your planting area.

Any side vines coming off of these primary vines
form a second group of vines which we will call
secondary vines. Many growers let these secondary
vines grow to their full potential without much fuss
or training while still other growers train these vines
so that they grow from the main vine in a perpendicular fashion. This eliminates criss-crossed vines,
and makes it easier to move freely between the secondaries to the primary vine for spraying and fertilizing. Using small bamboo sticks or light hold-
downs, these vines can be easily trained to go in the
direction you intend. Many believe that the secondaries are most important because they represent
more than 70% of the total leaf surface of the plant.

In New England, where thorough spraying for insects is a necessity, easy access to the interior of the plant is absolutely required; therefore, training of secondary vines must occur as soon as they start to trail. Each leaf axil could have a secondary vine, and they can occur every 18"-36" apart on the primary vine.

At some point in time, vegetative growth either naturally subsides, or it must be bridled so that maximum fruit growth is achieved. At this time,

(we will call these tertiary vines). Most growers pinch these immediately, thus eliminating criss-crossed vines, and reducing vegetative growth from all parts of the secondary vines — ends, as well as leaf axils.

The primary vine may be left to continue to grow — it will slow down quite naturally as the season progresses and the plant's growth emphasis shifts from vegetative to fruit development.

John Castellucci grew this symmetrical, 4-primary vine plant in 1997. Four fruit averaged over 600-pounds with the largest at 733 pounds.

secondary vines can be pruned. Based on what other successful growers have done, 6'-12' long secondary vines are ideal candidates for pruning. I attempt to utilize my growing area to the maximum, so I prune when secondaries reach the perimeter of my patch — which in all cases is less than 12'. These secondaries are "dead-headed" — simply put, the ends are chopped with a pointed shovel and then buried. Any new growth that appears from the ends of these vines is quickly pinched for the remainder of the season.

Before, and certainly after any secondary vines are dead-headed, a third group of vines will begin to emerge at leaf axils along the secondary vines

Many growers use the primary vine like a "valve" to control the growth of the fruit. If the fruit is growing too quickly, they will allow unbridled growth of the primary vine. If the fruit is lagging, they may dead-head the primary about 12'-15' after the set fruit. If all primaries and secondaries are dead-headed, and tertiaries are quickly pinched, then all energy must go into developing the fruit.

My observance is that the plant, many times, will do this on its own. Once the fruit begins to increase at a large rate, vegetative growth will naturally slow down, and many times, pruning of the primary vine is not necessary.

Fruits growing at alarming rates at the end of the season, that are in critical condition (stem stress, cracks or rings), can have this stress relieved by pruning much more severely to reduce the amount of energy going to the pumpkin. In this case, whole secondary vines are removed. With less leaves to manufacture energy, pumpkin growth should be slowed, reducing stress and the likelihood of catastrophic failure.

Pruning and vegetative growth management are not science — they are art. If you have an extremely large pumpkin in mid-August, get some help from a seasoned grower that has "ridden" one of these monsters from August to October. Help from people like Craig Weir of Salisbury, MA, Wayne Hackney of New Milford, CT or Joel Holland of Sumner, WA could help prevent a late season loss.

Vine Burying

Almost all competitive pumpkin growers do some vine burying during the season. Although some very large pumpkins have been grown without attention to the task of burying vines, most good growers still do it — and they do it for some very good and logical reasons. Burying vines helps to anchor them in position so they are less susceptible to wind damage. I've seen vines pinwheel, back and forth on the ground in 20 mile-an-hour winds, that eventually sever the vine from the rest of the plant. Burying vines also provides the necessary stability that fosters anchor root growth at each leaf axil. These anchor roots can provide a great deal of water and plant nutrients to the plant. There is a node on the bottom and top of the vine near each leaf axil that has the potential to sprout an anchor root. If you bury the vines, each of these nodes will sprout quicker. I once observed a plant that had been cut from its main root, which continued growing quite vigorously after a short period of adjustment. This was proof that anchor roots provide much to the plant.

Taking the burying of vines one step further is the cultural practice of mulching soil. I have observed in recent years the benefits of mulching. Not only does it provide the necessary weight to hold and anchor vines, but it also helps to preserve soil moisture, and most important, retards the emergence of weeds and grasses without the necessity of physical cultivation of the soil. It has become quite common knowledge that pumpkin plant roots spread far beyond the boundaries of their vines. Small, white, hair-like roots are easily damaged by even shallow cultivation. Mulching can almost eliminate the task of manual weed eradication, without any harmful effects.

You can mulch with many different materials, but none can compare with homemade compost. Compost not only serves as mulch but also as a constant, slow distributor of plant food. Your plants will flourish when mulched with compost.

I make my compost each year in the fall with fresh cow manure and leaf residue from my yard. By spring it is "black-gold." I used to spread it on my garden in early spring, and rototill it in before planting with another liberal dose of manure. Now I till-in just manure in early spring and save the compost for mulch. Eventually, it all makes its way into the soil.

Vine Patterns

The pattern that your plant makes on the ground has not been given much discussion over the years, but I have heard words used to describe various methods recently. These methods are generally used to either maximize garden space or streamline plant growth. Left to grow on its own, most plants would be a criss-cross of vines that would make access to the interior of the plant almost impossible.

Most growers begin training their plants from the time they begin to trail on the ground. Using hold-downs, sticks or soil, they position the ends of primary vines so that they go in the direction that they want. I have always used a 3 or 4 primary vine system where you train the main vine and 2 or 3 aggressive vines that emerge from the first 18" of vine in directions that are symmetrical to the plant's base. In this fashion, you have primary vines extending out in all directions for maximum use of your garden soil.

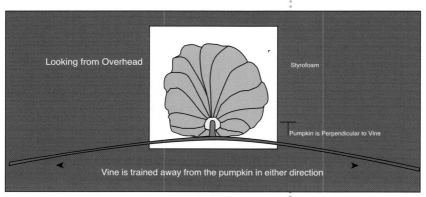

Another method relies on the use of a single primary vine and all tertiaries off of this vine are trained in a "Christmas tree" pattern to maximize growth of the plant in a given direction. This method is particularly useful in small gardens where growth must be controlled within a fairly constrained area. Placing transplants at the rear of an area and training them towards the front utilizes the garden space better. As the tertiaries reach the boundaries of the garden, they are severed and buried. Since the tip of the primary vine will have the newest growth, and shortest tertiaries off of it, dead-heading older tertiary vines tends to create a Christmas tree pattern. This method creates an aggressive primary vine which is an ideal candidate for growing a giant pumpkin.

Fruit Positioning

The way in which the pumpkin is positioned, in relationship to the vine, is very critical to a long and sustained season of fruit growth. Many pumpkins that develop stem stress midway through the season are the result of poor positioning, and many of these problems could be eliminated by careful modification of the fruit's position early in the growing season. There are cases where poor positions cannot be avoided. Occasionally you will see pumpkins in which the stem is directly beneath the growing fruit, and the blossom end points straight upward. This case usually produces flat, ill-shaped specimens (sometimes called "bird baths") that should be avoided or culled. Usually, no amount of repositioning of the fruit will remedy this case.

Early intervention will correct most of the potential bad fruit positions, and later severing of anchor roots around the fruit should be all that is required during the season to insure stress-free stems.

When a newly set fruit reaches basketball-size, its position in relationship to the stem should be evaluated. It should be as perpendicular to the vine as possible. Careful modification of position (about 1"-2" per day) over the course of a few days should get the fruit into its ideal position. Be very

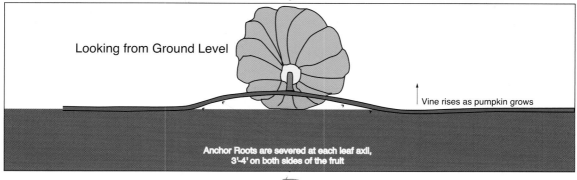

careful at this point of the season because stems are very fragile. Make small moves daily, and then brace the pumpkin's natural tendency to return to its original position by banking soil against the sides of the fruit. Always do this during the warmest part of the day when vines and stems are more relaxed and flexible. Trying to make even a small move on a cool, early morning, may result in damage.

Dick and Ron Wallace demonstrate a shade structure that allows easy access to their pumpkin.

You should visualize that the season ending position of the vine will show a slight rise as it approaches the pumpkin (see illustration on previous page), then gently fall as it resumes its growth on the other side of the fruit. This rise and fall is critical to relieving tension between the stem and vine. The vine should be loose, and have a little play in its movement in order to assure that stress is not occurring. This will not occur if you do not completely sever anchor roots on both sides of the fruit for several feet. Slide a sharp knife beneath the vine at a leaf axil, then gingerly with your hands, loosen the vine's hold on the soil. You will be amazed at how much this loosens the vine and how much it loosens the vine/stem tension.

Positioning the pumpkin perpendicular to the vine early in the season, and then severing anchor roots later are the two most important things you can do to relieve stem stress that will be inevitably encountered later in the season.

Fruit Shading

85% of 700-pound and over pumpkins grown in the world in 1996 and 1997 used some device to shade fruit to protect it from heat. This has become an almost universally accepted practice. Soon after the fruit reaches the size of a basketball, something should be erected that shades it from direct sunlight. It has been theorized that direct sunlight will overheat the pumpkin, possibly causing it to prematurely ripen before it has attained its full growth potential.

I have used 4' x 6' tarpaulins for years, securely attaching them to steel u-posts. I use 6' posts at the front (blossom-end) of the pumpkin and 4' posts at the rear (stem end). In this fashion, the tarp is

Right: John Snyder of Oxford, MA uses a worn sheet to shade his newly set pumpkins.

ground creates good shade and adequate space for continued air circulation. In this way, your pumpkin is not only shaded from the sun's heat, but also kept dry from rain and overhead watering.

angled to the stem-end to create good run-off of water and easy access from the front for measuring and inspection. You adjust posts so that the low end of the shade structure faces as much to the south as possible. The height of the tarp above

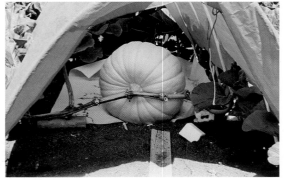

Protection Beneath the Fruit

Not all growers use protection below their pumpkins. This is more a matter of personal choice than an absolute must for growing a giant. A few years ago many growers were using 1" styrofoam cut into 2' x 2' pieces. These pieces are placed under the fruit when it is about the size of a basketball, and unless you have three arms, you will need some help to do this. I place this initial protection under the fruit and vine, so cutting of the tap root directly below the stem must be done at this time. Most use ground protection to keep the pumpkin as dry as possible throughout the season, and to prevent an invasion by moles or field mice from below. Just about any material can be used, but something pliable and flexible works better than material that is rigid and hard. As your pumpkin grows, additional pieces of material will be eventually needed on the sides and blossom-end of the pumpkin.

Top: Al Berard of Sanford, Maine, measures the circumference of the "stump." Notice the three, extremely stout primary vines.
Left: Two views of a Jack LaRue shade structure made from pvc piping and inexpensive tarpaulins.

Above: Paula McGeary shows-off a heavily rooted primary vine.
Right: Anchor roots grow from every leaf axil.
Below: Boards are used for traveling in and around the plant to reduce soil compaction.

Soil Compaction

It is advised that you do as little walking in your patch as possible. Treading on soil compacts the soil and retards maximum root growth, and the roots of pumpkin plants extend outward as much as 8'-10' from vines, so cultivating in these areas can do serious damage. Many growers place boards on common routes in the patch to prevent compaction, some have even created shoes, made to resemble snow shoes, that they wear while working in their gardens.

93

chapter eleven

Insidious Insects
& Demon Diseases

*Nothing can be more disheartening than an invasion
of Cucumber Beetles or Squash Vine Borers
and, nothing more dreaded than
the spores of pathological, demon diseases.*

You have to control insects and diseases if you expect to maximize the potential of your giant pumpkins. Since each grower's conditions may vary, there are no "chiseled in stone," decrees. Observation and experiment will ultimately determine your methods. I say this because there is a large segment of the growing community that feels strongly about spraying pesticides. I am the first to admit that if I did not have to spray, I would not. Anytime you put chemicals on the leaves or on the ground in the vicinity of your plant's roots, you expose the plant to some stress that can injure or slow its growth momentum. Ignoring certain insects that have an affinity for pumpkin plants will reduce your chances of growing a world class giant pumpkin, and may have season ending consequences for the plant. There are many totally organic gardeners growing giant pumpkins, but

none of them are breaking world records. If you decide to grow giant pumpkins and want to compete on a level playing field with top-echelon growers, you will eventually have to resort to some pesticide applications.

That said, let's discuss how we can do it in the least offensive way for the plant and the environment. The enemies are fairly common to most growers although some of you may encounter only some or none of the insects and diseases described. Some may even have more menacing pests, but high on the "hit list" of insidious insects and demon diseases are: Striped Cucumber Beetles, Squash Bugs and the Squash Vine Borer, and for diseases, Bacterial Wilt, Phytophthora, Powdery Mildew and Watermelon Mosaic Virus. How you combat these pests can fall into two application categories: spray and no-spray programs.

Striped Cucumber Beetles

This slim, 1/4" long yellow beetle with three black stripes running the length of its wings can, in numbers, completely consume young seedlings. They can appear anytime after soil begins to warm

The adult Squash Vine Borer has proven to be the most destructive insect effecting pumpkin growers. Although not found everywhere that pumpkins are grown, if they are present, they must be dealt with.

Above: A Striped Cucumber Beetle devours a tender pumpkin leaf.

Right: A Squash Vine Borer is found inside a pumpkin vine. By this time, the plant has suffered severely, and extraction is the only course of action.

as they pupate and emerge from soil they have overwintered in. Their control also holds the key in establishing control of bacterial wilt which they can spread from plant to plant during their eating frenzy. Since they over winter in the soil, frequent cultivation before the season can eliminate much of the immediate population, but since they will travel long distances to feast on cucurbits, other means must be employed to totally control them. On new transplants and small plants, a covering of floating row-cover material (Remay) will prevent beetles from reaching their intended prey. As plants become larger this becomes impractical and spraying with *Sevin* will have to be done on a routine basis. Endosulphan (*Thiodan*) can also be used. For organic growers, *Rotenone* does give fairly effective control.

Squash Bugs

This large bug, sometimes measuring .75" long, can do enormous damage to all vine crops and especially pumpkin plants. Commonly called the "Stink Bug" because of its odor when crushed, it lays brick-red eggs in masses or clusters on leaves. Eggs hatch out tiny nymph which have greenish brown bodies and reddish heads. Both nymph and adults are voracious eaters, with plants showing

extreme wilt from their presence. This wilting is the result of a toxic substance that the bug injects into the plant, and causes the eventual blackening of leaves. They can be controlled with normally used insecticides, and any program of spraying should be stepped up when egg masses are observed.

It has been my observation that most competitive pumpkin growers are using either *Sevin* or a systemic insecticide. Systemics like *Isotox* and *Merit* are not cleared or labeled for use on pumpkins, but that has not prevented competitive growers from taking advantage of their superior control. I cannot recommend that you use materials that are not cleared by your regulatory authorities, I can only tell you what others are using and have had fairly good control with. **You should obey the laws of your state concerning pesticide use.** Cabaryl *(Sevin)*, endosulphan *(Thiodan)*, methoxychlor and *Rotenone* are all cleared in most states.

Squash Vine Borers

The Squash Vine Borer is common to some parts of Southern Canada and the United States east of the Rocky Mountains. Its prey all seem to be among the Cucumber Family in which squash, gourds, cucumbers, melons and pumpkins belong.

Its life cycle is fairly simple, and a knowledge of it is essential in controlling its numbers. From egg to larvae to pupae to moth, the Squash Vine Borer lives a life in which it is ever changing in appearance. The female adult moth is about the size of a wasp with a greenish brown body, translucent wings, a red to orange striped abdomen and five spots positioned in a row down the length of her back. She moves with darting and flickering movements which are reminiscent of a dragon fly. She lays eggs singly on leaf stems and vines. These eggs are oval, flat and brownish. The eggs hatch out white larvae with brown heads which quickly bore into vines and begin to feed on the tissue inside. You can usually find evidence of them by looking for frass (excrement) and holes along the vine. This greenish-yellow frass is your first tip that you have an invader. Once you see this, you may not be able to control the borer with insecticides, and you may have to perform surgery on the vine to extract the borer. Once inside the vine, the borer is protected from chemical sprays. Plants plagued by vine borers soon wilt and die, while the larvae spin cocoons inside the vine in which to hibernate as pupae to await the next season.

These overwintering pupae are normally found in the top 1"–5" of soil and they will predictably emerge from the soil as adults between June 8th and the 15th in southern New England. They will emerge up to 3 weeks earlier in the South and somewhat later in the North. The important thing to understand is that their adult life is fairly short, perhaps 6–8 weeks. The emerging female will immediately begin laying eggs on stems and vines, and will continue for about 4–5 weeks. This means that effective control can be obtained if you are diligent during the egg-laying period. In southern New England, thoroughly spraying leaves, stems and vines from about June 10th until July 20th will give good control.

Most growers use either *Sevin* or *Methoxychlor* as the mainstay in their insecticide control programs. Endosulphan (*Thiodan*) and *Rotenone* are also used. All of these insecticides have short residual periods (the time in which they are active deterrents) so, they must be sprayed periodically and consistently throughout the growing season. A once-a-week spraying should give good control, with additional sprays required when excessive rain or overhead watering has washed chemical residues off of leaves and stems. Sprays should be directed at all of the plant parts, especially the leaf stems which seem to be the likely target of egg laying moths. Spraying should be done after the sun has begun to set in the evening. It is at this time that flower blossoms will begin to close and bees will be less active in the garden. *Sevin* is very toxic to bees, and any spraying during the day should be refrained. Spraying after 7–8 PM prevents insecticide from penetrating the interior of blossoms, since they are closed. When these blossoms open the following morning, bees will be free to roam in and out of them without coming in contact with the insecticide.

In place of *Sevin* or other chemical insecticides, some organic growers will use *Rotenone*, diatomaceous earth and *Bt*. They are fairly effective in controlling the larvae stage, but do nothing in hindering the adult in her egg laying activities. Since the Squash Vine Borer lays her eggs singly, the chances of finding all of these single egg locations are very slim. Once the larvae is inside the vine, only extraction can prevent it from totally killing that section of the vine. Extracting the borer can be as injurious to the plant as the borer itself, and much care must be taken to prevent the entrance of diseases into the plant's system after the extraction. It is better to prevent the borer from entering in the first place, and this can only be prevented by deterring the adult moths.

Other non-chemical procedures which will help in reducing borers are fairly simple practices. Since the pupae over-winter in the top 1"–5" of soil, frequent cultivation before planting will reduce their numbers later. Begin this in the Fall, and continue right up until planting. Also, burning infected vines will kill any active borers that are contained in them. These practices should be followed by any grower, regardless of using chemical or organic insecticides.

The end results of an invasion of dreaded phytophthora. Below (left and right): The symptoms of phyto are wilted leaves, mushy vines, then total death of the plant.

Bacterial Wilt

Bacterial Wilt is less common than other diseases affecting pumpkins, but can become a problem if you are prone to attacks from Cucumber Beetles. The bacteria cannot survive from one season to the next on infected debris. The bacteria proliferates and spreads by the feeding of Striped Cucumber Beetles. The beetles ingest the bacteria while eating the pumpkin's leaves or other host plants, then passes the disease to other leaves as they feed. The best control for Bacterial Wilt is a good insect control program which eliminates, or drastically reduces the population of Cucumber Beetles.

Phytophthora

It is not the 1950's and the invasion of the Japanese film makers. There are no Godzillas lumbering waist-deep in ocean water swatting planes like flies — no alien beings, no body-snatchers, no blobs, no creatures from the Black Lagoon. Yet,

it's faster than a speeding bullet, more powerful than a loco-motive, able to leap tall buildings in a single bound. Look, up in the sky, it's a bird, it's a plane... it's super spore – Phytophthora!

This is a fungus that is only detectable by microscope but can leave total devastation in its wake. Introduced to New England only a few years ago, it has already created a name for itself, "Phyto" for short — and has become a thorn in the side of commercial growers and chemical researchers who are driven to find something that will slow it down.

Yes, it attacks pumpkins with a vengeance, and because pumpkins are very low on the food chain, and lacking in commercial significance, this problem may get worse before it gets better. *Aliette,* which is not approved for use (but has been used by some competitive and commercial growers I have observed) is only fairly effective in the fight against this disease. The right weather conditions makes it all but impossible to control. Besides, *Aliette* is alarmingly expensive. One commercial grower says its cheaper to buy pumpkins from uninfected areas like New York and New Jersey than it is to plant, spray, and then hope that it will prevent an invasion in New England. In our area, the regulatory agency recommends spraying with *Ridomil/Bravo* and *Ridomil/Copper* but stresses limiting applications to just four times per year to minimize the potential of developing resistance to these fungicides.

Phyto is a plant fungus that causes severe wilting to leaves followed by mushy vines and stems. When this starts to happen, the season is generally over for the infected plant. Phyto leaves the vines of pumpkins like "cream of wheat." Vines turn to mush and pumpkins wither and die. Phyto attacks occur when you have extended periods of high humidity or rainy days.

Commercial growers, planting unprotected fields, are creating huge breeding grounds for these spores — and eventually they will make it to your patch. Wind, rain, birds, anything that moves can bring it to you. If you walk in an infected field, your shoes become a vehicle of transfer.

What can you do? Consult a regional specialist, preferably one with experience with diseases on cucurbits. Make contact and begin developing a relationship with people of this caliber. Practice good procedures by sterilizing tools used in pruning and cultivation. Knives, hoes, small tools, shovels, and gloves should all be sterilized with a mixture of bleach and water after every use. Experiment with some of the natural enemy spores like: Bio-Trek, Rootshield or T22 which colonize roots, preventing invasions by pathogenic diseases, and if you have the space, rotate pumpkins to new soil every 2-3 years.

As a final defense, fumigate soil. This should give you protection for a few years, but because "Phyto" is air-borne, you will have to repeat this procedure periodically. *Basamid* has been used by some growers in the Northeast. It is a granule that can be applied with a spreader to fully cultivated soil. You then must incorporate it by tilling again, then roll the soil to compact it. Dissolving it and keeping the ground wet for three days releases fumes that rids the soil of all diseases, weed seeds and insect larvae.

Powdery Mildew

Powdery Mildew appears as light yellow spots that eventually become covered by white spores. These spores give the appearance of powder on the leaf. Powdery Mildew can infect both sides of the leaves as well as stems. Infected plants develop yellowing leaves which eventually die. Infection takes place when high humidity conditions are present. The disease is especially active when high

Left: Powdery Mildew is one of these most common diseases found in late season giant pumpkins. Seaweed has been shown to prevent invasion.

densities of leaf growth prevent normal air flow from drying the plant's parts. Night time dew creates ideal conditions for its spread. Most growers use either *Benlate, Topsin* or *Bayleton. Benlate* and *Topsin* are in the same class of fungicide, so when using these products, it is advised that you alternate between *Bayleton* and either *Benlate* or *Topsin* (do not use both). Liquid seaweed, applied once a week to leaves, has also shown some promise in preventing infestations.

Watermelon Mosaic Virus WMV

This virus occurs when summer heat and high humidity combine during the growing season. With no effective control, precautions must be taken to undermine its initial attack. Perhaps planting somewhere else is the answer, because this soil borne spore over-winters readily, and any patch that has had this virus before, will have it again. It is spread by insects and garden tools. Symptoms include a yellowing between leaf veins

with the eventual deterioration of the entire leaf. Plants and fruit become extremely stunted.

Insect and Disease Control — A Necessary Evil

I have long encouraged the use of pesticides and fungicides in a normal program for growing giant pumpkins. Squash Vine Borers and Cucumber Beetles, along with a myriad of diseases from powdery mildew to bacterial wilt, have made it absolutely essential that some kind of concerted effort be made by a grower if any measure of success is to be obtained. The disappointing part about spraying chemicals on fragile, tender plants is that it is unnatural, and inevitably, some degree of injury is always sustained by the plant, each and every time

Top right and bottom left: Symptoms of the virus, Watermelon Mosaic (WMV).
Right: Symptoms of Cucumber Mosaic Virus (CMV) which is also fairly common among other cucurbits like giant pumpkins.

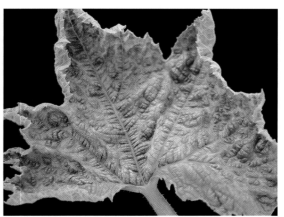

we spray. So, along with a steadfast commitment to controlling pests and diseases, we should also be keenly aware of the effects of our actions on the plants. In recent years, learning from my errors of the past, I have avoided spraying new foliage which was most susceptible to spray injury. The last 2'-3' of vine is very tender and any spray injury that occurs is bound to occur here.

I have, in the past, encouraged a strict regimen of spraying, particularly during the egg-laying period of the Squash Vine Borer. Having sustained a season-ending onslaught of this pest in 1994, I have been very protective of my plants ever since. This over protection has occasionally manifested itself with signs of stunted growth and curled and burnt leaf edges. I have always looked at this damage as a necessary evil in the fight to avoid a more dangerous situation.

In observing other competitive and commercial growers, I looked for pesticides and fungicides that were less severe on the pumpkin plants, yet were effective in controlling the problems. Ideally, I wanted to spray less with better results. What I observed was that some growers, that were having success, were using products that were not cleared or labeled by their state regulatory bodies. I cannot recommend that you do the same. I can only point out what others are using.

I felt that a calendar-format would be the best way to present this program, so the following pages

show the months of June, July, August and September with notations made in critical areas of the summer. It is important to understand that the dates are not absolutely perfect — they offer only a guide. Weather and your own observations will inevitably dictate when to commence spraying. The calendar does, however, address an artful rotation from contact to systemic sprays, and a thoroughly planned assault on pests, fungi, virus and bacterial infestations with great logic — "Oh, the things competitive pumpkin growers weave."

However, Isotox and Aliette are not labeled for the uses described in this calendar of spraying, and therefore, their use is not recommended.

Top left: Alternaria and fusarium wilt are both soil diseases which are difficult to prevent or control. Above: Black rot is quite common in pumpkins and is more prevalent where season long stress has reduced the fruit's resistance, or damage has occurred from either hail or mishandling which allows for its start.

JUNE

RIPGA
RHODE ISLAND PUMPKIN GROWERS ASSOCIATION
PEST MANAGEMENT PROGRAM

1999

SUNDAY	MONDAY	TUESDAY	WEDNESDAY	THURSDAY	FRIDAY	SATURDAY
		1 Sevin	2	3	4	5
Control of Cucumber Beetles starts when they first appear. They can ravage a small seedling in a single day, but that's not the worst of it. They spread Bacterial Wilt which will reduce your pumpkin growing potential. This program recommends Sevin as a spot killer.						
6	7	8	9 Isotox	10	11	12
Control of the Adult Squash Vine Borer begins this week. Isotox, a systemic insecticide, is not specifically cleared for pumpkins or edible fruits and vegetables, so if you choose to use this product, you must not allow the fruit, flowers or seeds to be used as food. If you plan to use this spray program, this is a responsibility that you must accept in order to assure safety. You may substitute Sevin or Methoxychlor in place of Isotox.						
13	14	15	16	17	18	19 Sevin
20	21	22	23 Isotox	24	25	26
27	28	29	30			

JULY

RIPGA
RHODE ISLAND PUMPKIN GROWERS ASSOCIATION
PEST MANAGEMENT PROGRAM

1999

SUNDAY	MONDAY	TUESDAY	WEDNESDAY	THURSDAY	FRIDAY	SATURDAY
				1	2	3
4	5	6	7 Isotox	8	9	10 Ridomil Kocide
Humidity and moist soil conditions can begin now, and the chances for the spread of disease escalates. Preventing disease is much easier than eliminating it, so start early and spray often. If you have not experienced a Phytophthora infestation, Ridomil and Aliette can be eliminated from this spray schedule. Remember, "When it rains it spores," so work your spray program around precipitation and high humidity periods.						
11	12	13	14	15	16	17
18	19	20 Ridomil Kocide	21 Isotox	22	23	24
25	26	27	28	29	30	31

AUGUST

RIPGA
RHODE ISLAND PUMPKIN GROWERS ASSOCIATION
PEST MANAGEMENT PROGRAM

1999

SUNDAY	MONDAY	TUESDAY	WEDNESDAY	THURSDAY	FRIDAY	SATURDAY
1	2	3	4	5	6 Ridomil Manzate	7
8	9	10	11 Isotox	12	13	14
15	16 Ridomil Kocide	17	18	19	20	21
22	23	24	25 Isotox	26 Ridomil Bravo	27	28 Aliette Benlate
29	30	31				

Aliette is not labeled or cleared for use on pumpkins, so I cannot recommend this fungicide.
Some commercial growers have had fairly good success with it in controlling Phytophthora. If you have no symptoms of Phytophthora, eliminate it from consideration as a component of your spray program for disease.

SEPTEMBER

RIPGA
RHODE ISLAND PUMPKIN GROWERS ASSOCIATION
PEST MANAGEMENT PROGRAM

1999

SUNDAY	MONDAY	TUESDAY	WEDNESDAY	THURSDAY	FRIDAY	SATURDAY
			1 Isotox	2 Ridomil Manzate	3	4 Aliette Benlate
5	6	7	8	9 Ridomil Kocide	10	11
12	13	14	15	16	17	18 Aliette Benlate
19	20	21	22	23	24	25
26	27	28	29	30		

The likelihood of a frost during this period will allow you to suspend spraying for the season. If you do not get a frost, or you are erecting a canopy over your plant to extend the season, continue spraying using the same schedule.

The No-Spray Program

This insect and disease program is not for everyone because it is a radical use of existing materials that have undergone only limited testing with giant pumpkins. I feel strongly that competitive pumpkin growers who experience damage from insects and diseases can benefit from this less time-consuming, less offensive method. Anytime you spray chemicals directly onto the leaves of pumpkin plants, you run the risk of injury, or at the least, a slowdown in the momentum of the plant's growth. At the heart of this method is the basic premise that pesticides applied to the ground are less offensive to the plant than those applied directly to its leaves.

As a competitive pumpkin grower, you must spray insecticides and fungicides early and often to keep plants free from invasion. The key problem in this strategy is the effect that these toxic sprays have on our plants. On occasion, I have burnt leaves (particularly new growth) and have always been apprehensive that if damage can occur on occasion, then perhaps we are reducing the overall vitality of the plant with each and every spray we make – even if we do not observe any damage to the plant.

In the search for alternative materials, I looked for growers that were using materials that were longer lasting, had more residual activity, were systemic in nature, and could be applied to the ground around plants (rather than to the leaves). In addition, I wanted to use materials that were relatively safe and readily available to home owners. If you need a pesticide license to purchase a material, it doesn't make sense to include it here for the general population of competitive pumpkin growers.

I focused on a program that would include a systemic insecticide granule that could be applied to the soil in early spring and give good control of our problems through harvest. For those experiencing root diseases, I wanted a material that could be applied less frequently than the once-a-week fungicide programs that stress a multitude of

materials to compete against mutating fungi. I have found just such materials, but I stress that none of these has seen extensive testing with pumpkins. Under these circumstances, if you use this program, it is imperative that you control the use of your pumpkins after harvest. The insecticide component of this program, *Merit,* is not labeled for use on pumpkins. Although it has been cleared in New England for use on potatoes against the voracious Colorado Potato Beetle, **no pumpkin that you grow using this program should be sold or given away where the possibility of it being eaten exists. This is a precaution that must be adhered to if you use this method. I cannot recommend the use of *Merit* in any spray program for pumpkins.**

Merit (also known by its chemical name, Imidacloprid) is available at virtually every garden and home center in the US. Promoted for use as a grub control in lawns, it is sold as a granule that can be applied to turf at anytime of the year – giving systemic protection for the entire season. The normal concentration is .2% to .3% Imidacloprid, and the recommendation for control of Japanese Beetle grubs is 2-3 lbs. per 1000 square feet. 1000 square feet is roughly the size of a mature giant pumpkin plant. You can apply *Merit* to your pumpkin patch with a broadcast spreader. Follow the directions on the bag for use against grubs, using the spreader settings indicated. Apply in early season so that natural rainfall can dissolve the material and get it into the root zone of the plant prior to planting. Applications anytime in April or May should work. In addition, another treatment in early June is advised to insure good uptake for the onslaught of the Squash Vine Borer.

Be forewarned that if you observe damage from insects that is beyond a reasonable expectation, then you may have to supplement with a spot spray with the customary insecticides used. *Merit* should get you through the season without spraying any insecticides on the leaves of your plants, freeing you to do other things. You will also not have to perform the arduous task of delivering spray materials to the underside of leaves, leaf stems and vines — thus reducing foot traffic in the patch around highly susceptible root zones. Since *Merit* is a systemic, insects must eat the plant to be affected by the pesticide. It will control Striped Cucumber Beetles, but a particularly large invasion may have to be met with a spray of *Sevin*. But, observe carefully before you spray. It is better to not spray than to spray.

Bio-Trek, Rootshield and T22 are all EPA-registered fungicide products for control of plant diseases that affect roots. All contain a fungus called *Trichoderma harzianum* that colonizes plant roots preventing plant pathogens from causing root diseases such as Pythium and Phytophthora. Essentially, their activity is so aggressive that other pathogens cannot compete with them. In fact, *Trichoderma* can be a parasite of many of these pathogens — attaching themselves to them, and literally sucking the life out of them. They last the entire season. This material should be applied in April or May, and then thoroughly incorporated into the soil with a rototiller.

The use of Bio-Trek, Rootshield or T22 should completely eliminate most of the root diseases affecting pumpkins, but if the need arises, other fungicides can be used on an as-needed basis. Most fungicides are compatible with these materials. In addition, *Rootshield* produces healthier root systems, and this will translate into much healthier plants. *Rootshield* is available in 5 and 10 pound boxes. Broadcast at the rate of 2 pounds per 1000 square feet, then till into soil.

Additional No-Spray Considerations

Zero Tolerance is a revolutionary new horticultural product that offers a new tool in the fight against infectious diseases. It cleans plants, fruit, equipment and growing facilities of all pathogenic microorganisms and their spores that cause horticultural infectious diseases.

It decontaminates plant tissue from harmful fungi, bacteria and virus without damaging plant tissue, fruit or flowers. It cleans not only fungi, but the spores that cause them. It can be applied at anytime during the season but precautions should be taken on extremely hot days..

Essentially it is the "Lysol" of the plant world. Great for occasional decontamination and cleanup before, during and after those times of the season when diseases can become highly active. Spray during prolonged periods of rainfall or high humidity. This product will serve you well if used during July and August. I include it in the no-spray program as an additional consideration. You are, after all, spraying it on the leaves and ground, but it will cause absolutely no adverse effects on the plant. If it can be sprayed on young, greenhouse seedlings, it is safe for maturing pumpkin plants. *Zero Tolerance* can be used as a tool in fighting the spread of infectious plant diseases when they are encountered. It is available in 1 gallon containers. Apply at the rate of 1 ounce per gallon to upper and lower leaf surfaces on a biweekly basis starting when heat and humidity produce ideal conditions for development of fungi.

Except for rare occasions using the no-spray program, you will have only limited use of your trusted tool, the compression sprayer.

chapter twelve

Critter Control

Whether it be field mice, rabbits, possum, raccoons or the dreaded woodchuck, garden varmints can break the morale of even the most dedicated giant pumpkin grower. Obsessive behavior is likely to be exhibited.

I am not anti-animal, nor do I spend too much of my time concocting schemes that are bent on destruction of little critters, however, like any competitive pumpkin grower, I take the protection of my plants very seriously. Every grower feels the frustration of battling a semi-nocturnal invader in the patch. If you've ever been rudely awakened from one of your morning excursions to the patch by the absence of ends to your primary and secondary vines, you know the feeling every grower feels when he knows that a woodchuck has discovered his pumpkin plants.

I once saw a bumper sticker that read, "You know you're alone when the kids have finally left home, and the cats have all died." But I would add... "and the chucks have all gone north for the summer!" I have battled the woodchuck for fifteen years now, and any dent that I have made in their population does not seem evident. It's like counting sheep in an endless nightmare. Where do they all come from?

The Woodchuck has become my arch enemy in the fight to determine who will rule the pumpkin patch!

During the spring and summer months, almost all serious, competitive pumpkin growers obsess about the dawn and dusk raids of the varmint of the underground. I've had an ongoing hate-affair with this critter which has decimated many a vegetable garden with its obese appetite for new greens, lush shoots, and tender seedlings. Broccoli, beans and peas, at an early stage of their development, seem like magnets for this slow, tentative, eating-machine.

In recent years, with an increased emphasis placed on growing giant pumpkins, it seems the local breed of chuck has developed a fond-liking for the ends of pumpkin vines. It's been an acquired taste by a more resolute, and obviously, more intelligent animal. "Survival of the fittest," and the intelligent shall survive in the Langevin corner of the planet. My woodchucks have evolved into mutant snipers with appetite disorders.

I must confess, my dogged attempts at eliminating this pesky critter has probably done more harm than good. I've trapped, rifled, drowned and speared at least a hundred over the last decade, but each year, one or two seem to evade all the tactics I employ in their destruction. The result is genetic selection which preserves the brightest and most intelligent for annual reproduction. Each year, the warfare becomes harder and more difficult to control. Each year, I have a more formidable adversary. After all this, I do not claim to have any affection or sympathy for the balance of nature in respects to this member of the food-chain.

My favorite comedy-movie of all time, therefore, has to be *Caddy Shack*. It combines the game of golf (which I love very much), with a totally berserk crusade against the groundhogs of an exclusive country club. If you've never seen it, go out and rent a copy today. Bill Murray plays the part of a half-witted assistant greens keeper who is given the task of eliminating a menacing groundhog. Murray tries to shoot, drown, and ultimately blow-up the critter. But alas, the golf course and Murray lose, and the 'chuck dances to the music of Kenny Loggins. There is no comedy in my pursuits, but it is a pure, Bill Murray effort — with results that mostly resemble comedy. As many as I eliminate, they still remain, dancing to the music.

I've traded stories with many gardeners over the years — each with his own strategy for ridding their gardens, once and for all, of the woodchuck. Each that I've met still has an enduring frustration at its presence. I once listened to three as they discussed a delicate question — "What do you do with the woodchucks you trap in your *Havahart* trap?" A *Havahart* trap catches critters alive. What you do with them after is your business. The manufacturer presumes that you release them unharmed. Any realist knows "That ain't necessarily so." Having heard the same question myself, I listened to the three. The first grower said, "I drown them in a nearby pond. They don't swim very well underwater in a cage." The second grower said, "I take them into the barn and spear them with a hayfork. They don't move very quickly in the cage." And the third grower said, "I don't have the heart to do any of that. I just let them starve to death in the trap."

It's a wacky world we live in, and you may be saying, these three are cruel and abusive of God's creations. I must remind you that in Minnesota last year, a pit-bull ripped the hand from a four-year-old neighbor's child. The enraged father promptly beat the dog to within an inch of its life with a baseball bat. The townspeople started two, simultaneous fund raisers. One was for the medical bills involved in reconstructing the little girl's hand, and the other was for veterinary bills involved with the pit-bull's recuperation. The little girl's fund raiser raised $800, the dog got more than $10,000 in donations.

In all my years, fences have not stopped the woodchuck, including electrified fortifications. The use of ultrasonic sound was foolishness. If you make a better woodchuck trap, people will buy it — but that doesn't mean that it will actually work. Chewing gum clogs their digestive systems, or so I've heard. One year a ten-pack of Wrigley's Spearmint disappeared, a stick at a time, from the back of my patch. That year I bought more gum for the chucks than I did for my kids! I don't know if it worked. It may be that the smart chucks don't like spearmint, and much prefer Bazooka. For that matter, I feed more apples to the chucks as bait for my trap than I feed to my kids. During the summer, our house is never without a fresh, Granny Smith apple — for the woodchucks. Smoke bombs have not reduced their numbers. One year I deposited a gross of bombs into craters in my backyard. After thirty minutes of bombing, I looked-up and suddenly realized what Stephen Crane was describing in his classic *Red Badge of Courage*. The Civil War battlefield could not have looked much differently than this. The smoke lingered two to three feet off the ground, the smell of sulfur stung my nostrils — I could hear the canons and the cavalry.

A friend once told me of the Rat Terrier. This very small English-breed of dog, when properly trained, will actually go down into the woodchuck's burrow and retrieve it, then quickly take its life. I can't imagine a dog, smaller than a woodchuck, with such spunk and nerve. I wonder if he eats little kid's hands?

Other Critters to Contend With

Depending on where you live, any one of these animals can present problems when growing giant pumpkins. In most cases, with possums, wood-chucks, skunks, rabbits or raccoons, you can capture them in traps baited with sour apples. Field mice cannot be totally eliminated, but protecting the bottom of your fruit with a ground covering, like styrofoam, will prevent them from burrowing under your prize and turning its inside into their own personal condo and restaurant.

In the case of deer, only sturdy, high fencing will deter them from your patch if they are hungry. They particularly like pumpkin seeds, so the sure sign that you have damage from deer will be smashed pumpkins, which they accomplish by stomping with their hoofs.

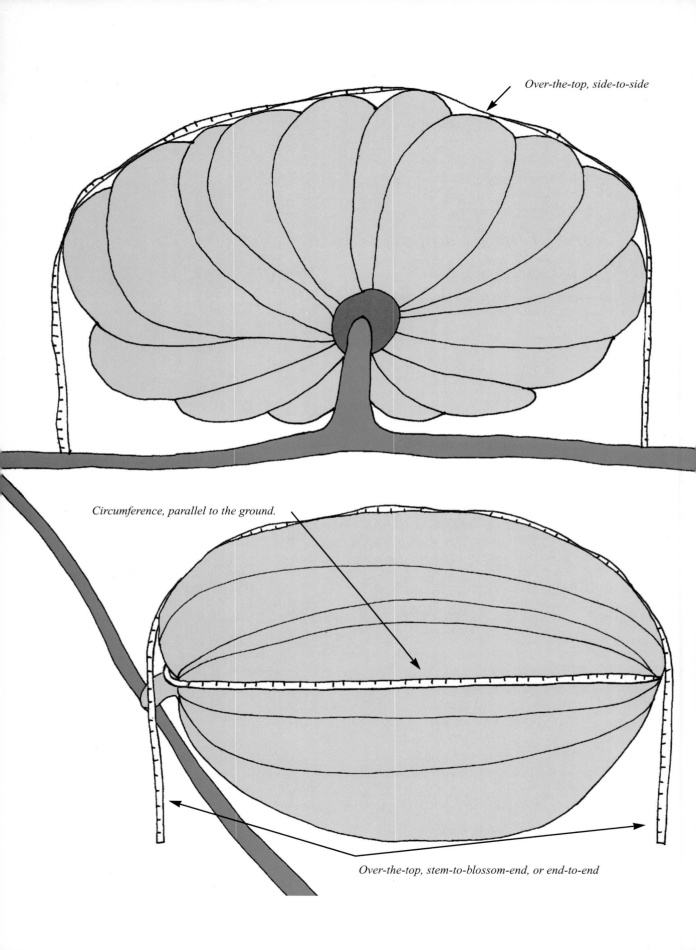

Over-the-top, side-to-side

Circumference, parallel to the ground.

Over-the-top, stem-to-blossom-end, or end-to-end

chapter thirteen
Estimating Weight

One of the joys of growing a giant pumpkin is watching it get larger day-by-day. Thanks to Bob Marcellus, we have a table that can convert measurements into a fairly precise estimate of weight.

ob Marcellus will have your head spinning just minutes after talking to him. He speaks a language we are all vaguely familiar with, but somehow lost full conception of when our math careers collided with our first calculus course.

The good thing is that you do not have to understand algebra, geometry, physics or statistics to estimate your pumpkin's weight. Bob has done most of the work, and with linear extrapolations, (pardon the expression), he has made the act of determining the weight of a giant pumpkin as simple as measuring your pumpkin and comparing the results to his table at the end of this chapter. There are, however, a few things you have to understand before wagering your home on an estimated world record pumpkin.

As the seasoned, giant pumpkin grower would tell you, "It doesn't weigh anything until it gets on a scale." This attitude comes from years of pre-weigh off suspense that was followed by disap-

Over-the-Top measurements are far more accurate than just using the circumference only, but the circumference measurement can be taken daily, and it will easily give a quick reference to weight gains.

pointment at the annual event. Most of the time, the table is fairly accurate (+ or - 5%), but occasionally surprises will occur.

Getting a good estimate of weight is a function of making good measurements, and then making observations of the shape of your pumpkin. Tall pumpkins tend to weigh more than their estimated weight, as do pumpkins that have most of the bulk of their volume on the stem end of the pumpkin. Pumpkins with shiny, tender skin tend to weigh less than their estimated weight while those that are gnarled and mottled tend to weigh more. Those that are covered by a late season netting, similar to that which occurs on the skin of cantaloupes, tend to weigh more than their estimated weight (this condition being referred to as cantalouping). Pumpkins with big, well-defined ribs tend to weigh more than their estimated weights while those that are less defined weigh less. These are just casual observations without any empirical data to confirm or deny them, but you will find all competitive growers using one of these observations, from time-to-time, to justify why he thinks his pumpkin will ultimately weigh more than its estimated weight.

So how do you get the best estimate of weight? Make your measurements correctly, compare them to the table, then add and deduct 5% of the estimated weight to create a range of weight. In this way, you'll be taking into account under estimates and over estimates of the actual weight.

How-To Measure Correctly

Good measurements can be very difficult to make as your pumpkin bulks-up in mid to late August. I take a measurement of the circumference every day to track daily growth, and use the Over-the-Top Method on a weekly basis to track estimated weight. The daily circumference measurements tell me if my pumpkin's growth is slowing or accelerating. I have kept daily diaries for the past four years, so it is nice to compare my present pumpkin with pumpkins that have actually made it to the scale. Each Sunday, I take three measurements, in what is called the Over-the-Top Method of estimating weight. The first measurement is circumference, and is taken from stem to blossom end, holding the tape parallel to the ground (attempting to get the biggest possible measurement). This will become a chore at advanced stages of the season, and a helping hand will go a

long way in holding the tape in place as you encircle your pumpkin. The second measurement is taken over-the-top, side-to-side. It is important that the tape go straight-up on one side and straight down from the widest point on the other side. (See the illustrations on this page for the correct position of the tape.) The third measurement is taken over-the-top, end-to-end (or stem to blossom end). The same procedures should be followed in making this measurement. You now have three measurements. Add them together, and find their sum in the table at the end of this chapter. If your pumpkin had a circumference of 140", a side-to-side measurement of 90" and an end-to-end measurement of 85", their sum would be 315" (140 + 90 + 85 = 315). When you find 315" on the table, you will see the weight of 625 lbs. next to it. As a comparison, find the circumference only measurement on the other table. Next to 140" you will find the weight of 597 lbs. For this example, let's use the over-the-top table and apply the 5% under and over method to create a range of weight. In this case, a pumpkin with total measurements of 315" would have an estimated weight of 594 to 656 lbs. (625 x .95 = 594 and 625 x 1.05 = 656).

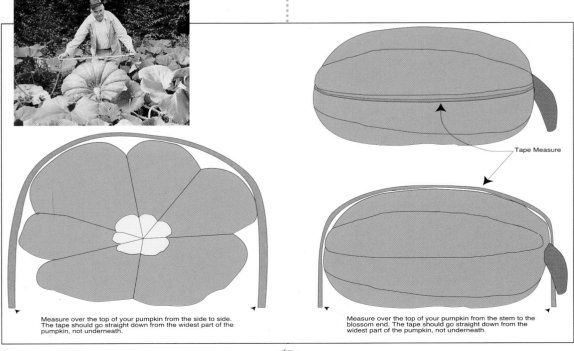

Measure over the top of your pumpkin from the side to side. The tape should go straight down from the widest part of the pumpkin, not underneath.

Measure over the top of your pumpkin from the stem to the blossom end. The tape should go straight down from the widest part of the pumpkin, not underneath.

Glen Brown's Tale of the Tape

As I said earlier, I am constantly comparing weekly measurements with pumpkins I have grown in previous years, and as an added incentive, I like to compare them with other growers' best efforts (when the data is available). Glen Brown's 1994, 923-pounder is shown here as a good example of an early, fast growing giant pumpkin.

	TOTAL MEASUREMENTS	ESTIMATED WEIGHT LBS.	LBS. GAINED FOR WEEK
July 30	234"	271	
Aug 6	284"	450	179
Aug 13	306"	556	106
Aug 20	323"	655	99
Aug 27	336"	743	88
Sept 3	344"	807	64
Sept 10	351"	870	63
Sept 17	354"	900	30
Sept 24	356"	920	20
Sept 29	357"	930	10

Oct 1   Actual Weight   923

Below: Glen Brown and his daughter, Amber, with his 1994, then U.S. record, 923-pounder.

Geneva Emmons' Tale of the Tape

Geneva's pumpkin diary is shown to demonstrate a pumpkin that grew later in the season. Notice that her biggest weight-gain week was August 20th thru the 28th and that late September weight gains were twice those of Glen Brown's 923. The 939 was pollinated on July 8th, while the 923 was pollinated on July 10th.

	TOTAL MEASUREMENTS	ESTIMATED WEIGHT LBS.	LBS. GAINED FOR WEEK
Aug. 13	273"	405	
Aug. 20	303"	561	156
Aug. 28	336.5"	749	188
Sept. 3	352.5"	852	103
Sept. 10	362"	917	65
Sept. 17	370.5"	977	60
Sept. 25	378"	1033	56
Sept. 27	379.5"	1044	11

Oct 5   Actual Weight   939

Below: Geneva and Don Emmons with their 1995, 939-pound pumpkin which was second in the world.

James Kuhn's Tale of the Tape

The 929.4 is the largest pumpkin ever grown in New England and this chart demonstrates its late start but tremendous growth right up to harvest. The 929.4 was pollinated on July 12th which is slightly later than the golden zone of July 1-10th. The seed was started on April 26th and transplanted to the garden cold frame on May 10th.

	TOTAL MEASUREMENTS	ESTIMATED WEIGHT LBS.	LBS. GAINED FOR WEEK
Aug. 6	203"	186	
Aug. 13	251"	335	149
Aug. 20	293"	510	175
Aug. 27	319"	650	140
Sept. 3	337"	750	100
Sept. 10	347"	820	70
Sept. 17	357"	880	60
Sept. 27	365"	938	58

Oct 4   Actual Weight   929.4

Al Eaton's 9-Year Averages

The table below shows the averages for Al Eaton's largest pumpkins, at the time of measurement, for a nine year period. This is valuable information from which all growers can draw conclusions on how well they are doing with their own pumpkin at any given time of the growing season.

Event	Date
Seed started	May 2
Germination	May 6
First true leaf	May 8
Transplanted	May 11
Five true leaves	May 22
1' vine	June 4
4' vine	June 13
6' vine	June 18
First male blossom	June 24
First female blossom	July 3
15" circumference	July 12
30" circumference	July 17
50" circumference	July 22
70" circumference	July 28
90" circumference	Aug. 2
110" circumference	Aug. 14
120" circumference	Aug. 21
130" circumference	Aug. 31

Below: Hugh Wiberg congratulates James Kuhn for his 1997, 929.4-pound pumpkin.

Below: Al Eaton hoists an 853-pound pumpkin with a homemade winch in 1997.

Over-the-Top Method for Estimating Weight

Total	Wgt	180	133	216	221	252	337	288	488	312	608	330	710	348	822	366	945	384	1079
50	4	181	135	217	223	253	341	289	493	312½	611	330½	713	348½	826	366½	949	384½	1083
55	5	182	137	218	226	254	345	290	497	313	614	331	716	349	829	367	952	385	1087
60	6	183	140	219	229	255	349	291	502	313½	617	331½	719	349½	832	367½	956	385½	1091
65	8	184	142	220	232	256	352	292	507	314	619	332	722	350	836	368	960	386	1095
70	10	185	144	221	235	257	356	293	512	314½	622	332½	725	350½	839	368½	963	386½	1099
75	12	186	146	222	238	258	360	294	516	315	625	333	728	351	842	369	967	387	1103
80	14	187	148	223	241	259	364	295	521	315½	627	333½	731	351½	846	369½	970	387½	1107
85	17	188	150	224	244	260	368	296	526	316	630	334	734	352	849	370	974	388	1111
90	20	189	153	225	247	261	372	297	531	316½	633	334½	737	352½	852	370½	978	388½	1115
95	23	190	155	226	250	262	376	298	536	317	636	335	740	353	856	371	981	389	1118
100	26	191	157	227	253	263	380	299	541	317½	639	335½	743	353½	859	371½	985	389½	1122
105	30	192	159	228	256	264	384	300	546	318	641	336	747	354	862	372	989	390	1126
110	34	193	162	229	259	265	388	300½	549	318½	644	336½	750	354½	866	372½	992	390½	1130
115	39	194	164	230	262	266	392	301	551	319	647	337	753	355	869	373	996	391	1134
120	44	195	166	231	265	267	396	301½	554	319½	650	337½	756	355½	872	373½	1000	391½	1138
125	49	196	169	232	269	268	400	302	556	320	653	338	759	356	876	374	1003	392	1142
130	54	197	171	233	272	269	404	302½	559	320½	655	338½	762	356½	879	374½	1007	392½	1146
135	60	198	173	234	275	270	408	303	561	321	658	339	765	357	883	375	1011	393	1151
140	67	199	176	235	278	271	412	303½	564	321½	661	339½	768	357½	886	375½	1015	393½	1155
145	73	200	178	236	282	272	417	304	566	322	664	340	771	358	889	376	1018	394	1159
150	81	201	181	237	285	273	421	304½	569	322½	667	340½	774	358½	893	376½	1022	394½	1163
152	84	202	183	238	288	274	425	305	572	323	670	341	778	359	896	377	1026	395	1167
154	87	203	186	239	292	275	429	305½	574	323½	672	341½	781	359½	900	377½	1030	395½	1171
156	90	204	188	240	295	276	434	306	577	324	675	342	784	360	903	378	1033	396	1175
158	93	205	191	241	298	277	438	306½	579	324½	678	342½	787	360½	907	378½	1037	396½	1179
160	96	206	193	242	302	278	443	307	582	325	681	343	790	361	910	379	1041	397	1183
162	100	207	196	243	305	279	447	307½	585	325½	684	343½	793	361½	914	379½	1045	397½	1187
164	103	208	199	244	309	280	451	308	587	326	687	344	797	362	917	380	1049	398	1191
166	107	209	201	245	312	281	456	308½	590	326½	690	344½	800	362½	921	380½	1052	398½	1195
168	110	210	204	246	316	282	460	309	592	327	693	345	803	363	924	381	1056	399	1200
170	114	211	207	247	319	283	465	309½	595	327½	696	345½	806	363½	928	381½	1060	399½	1204
172	118	212	209	248	323	284	469	310	598	328	699	346	810	364	931	382	1064	400	1208
174	121	213	212	249	326	285	474	310½	600	328½	701	346½	813	364½	935	382½	1068	400½	1212
176	125	214	215	250	330	286	479	311	603	329	704	347	816	365	938	383	1072	Table courtesy	
178	129	215	218	251	334	287	483	311½	606	329½	707	347½	819	365½	942	383½	1075	of Bob Marcellus	

Circumference Method for Estimating Weight

Circ.	Wgt	77	130	102½	274	116½	382	133	540	147	702	161	890	166½	972	172	1058	177½	1149
50	42	78	134	103	277	117	387	133½	546	147½	708	161½	898	167	980	172½	1066	178	1158
51	44	79	138	103½	281	120	413	134	551	148	715	162	905	167½	988	173	1075	178½	1166
52	46	80	143	104	284	120½	418	134½	557	148½	721	162½	912	168	995	173½	1083	179	1175
53	49	81	148	104½	288	121	422	135	562	149	727	163	920	168½	1003	174	1091	179½	1183
54	51	82	153	105	291	121½	427	135½	567	149½	734	163½	927	169	1011	174½	1099	180	1192
55	54	83	158	105½	295	122	431	136	573	150	740	164	935	169½	1019	175	1107	180½	1201
56	56	84	163	106	299	122½	436	136½	578	150½	747	164½	942	170	1027	175½	1116	181	1209
57	59	85	168	106½	302	123	441	137	584	151	753	165	949	170½	1034	176	1124	181½	1218
58	62	86	173	107	306	123½	445	137½	590	151½	760	165½	957	171	1042	176½	1132	182	1227
59	65	87	178	107½	310	124	450	138	595	152	766	166	965	171½	1050	177	1141	182½	1236
60	67	88	184	108	314	124½	455	138½	601	152½	773								
61	70	89	189	108½	317	125	460	139	606	153	779								
62	74	90	195	109	321	125½	464	139½	612	153½	786								
63	77	91	200	109½	325	126	469	140	618	154	793								
64	80	92	206	110	329	126½	474	140½	624	154½	800								
65	83	93	212	110½	333	127	479	141	630	155	806								
66	87	94	218	111	337	127½	484	141½	635	155½	813								
67	90	95	224	111½	341	128	489	142	641	156	820								
68	94	96	230	112	345	128½	494	142½	647	156½	827								
69	97	97	237	112½	349	129	499	143	653	157	834								
70	101	98	243	113	353	129½	504	143½	659	157½	841								
71	105	99	250	113½	357	130	509	144	665	158	848								
72	109	100	256	114	361	130½	514	144½	671	158½	855								
73	113	100½	260	114½	365	131	519	145	677	159	862								
74	117	101	263	115	370	131½	525	145½	683	159½	869								
75	121	101½	267	115½	374	132	530	146	690	160	876								
76	125	102	270	116	378	132½	535	146½	696	160½	883								

Above: Many thanks to Bob Marcellus for his tables for estimating pumpkin weights.

chapter fourteen

Murphy's Law

"If it can go wrong, it will." So goes one of the sayings of Murphy's Law. From stem splits to Dill rings to premature ripening, if you've got a big one going, don't expect it to be a "cake-walk" to the weigh off.

Getting a world class giant pumpkin to a weigh off is an agonizing, emotional affair fraught with feelings of apprehension, anxiety and impending doom. When a pumpkin is large enough for you to begin believing that you have something special, suddenly thoughts of doubt start to creep into your mind. For every story of a large pumpkin, there are tens, if not hundreds more, of the ones that "got away." From mid-August to the weigh offs in October, a host of problems can present themselves. Most of these problems are predictable if you know the genetic predisposition of a particular seed stock. All of them can occur, in any case, when growing an *Atlantic Giant* pumpkin. Some can be alleviated, and some you must sweat-out until weigh off day. Along the way to growing a world class giant pumpkin, you will come across most of the problems presented here. Luck has a lot to do with whether you encounter any of them, and whether you survive them. It's the Murphy Law that states, "If it can go wrong, it probably will."

A giant pumpkin under siege from catastrophic stem failure has splits which radiate into the fleshy ribs of the pumpkin. They must be quickly dried and hardened to reduce the chance of premature rotting of the fruit.

Dill Rings

I don't really know how this term came into being but I first heard it in 1995, and since, it has become universally accepted among competitive growers. In recent years, Dill rings have become almost as catastrophic as stem splits in ending the season of a fast-growing pumpkin.

A Dill ring is an internal crack that shows externally as an indentation running from side-to-side across the direction of the ribs. This indentation is the thinnest part of the pumpkin's walls. Generally, the stem end of the pumpkin will have the thickest walls, and the blossom end the thinnest walls. Dill rings that run across the blossom end are particularly more dangerous, but a Dill ring, anywhere on the pumpkin has season ending consequences.

The walls are also thinnest where each rib rolls inward. In maturing pumpkins, these deep crevices will have a wall thickness of 2"-3" less than the thickest part of the rib's walls. So, it is at the intersection of these crevices and a Dill ring where wall thicknesses are the absolute thinnest. With a sudden burst of growth, these areas can quickly open up — exposing the inside cavity to air, and a hastened end to the season.

(The pictures on these pages help to demonstrate a classic Dill ring. Note the large, angular crack in the internal wall in the photo inset on page 119. Although this Dill ring did not break through, you can see that at this point the structural framework was the weakest.)

You cannot avoid Dill rings altogether. Your probability of encountering them is reduced by growing seeds from *Atlantic Giant* stocks that have no noticeable Dill rings. Once you have a pumpkin with a Dill ring, not much can be done. Some growers have discontinued the use of fertilizers with hope that the slowed-down plant will not exert additional stress on the fast-growing pumpkin. Where size and weight is everything — turning off the "juice" is harder said than done.

Stem Splits

Stem splits are by far the most common problems that can occur while growing a giant pumpkin. It is also the most threatening to continued sound growth, but many growers have been able to deal successfully with stem splits with a regimen of care and adjustment of fruit position. The worst stem splits do not occur on the stem but rather into the flesh of the pumpkin at the junction of where the stem attaches to the fruit. These splits will radiate-out from the stem in the deepest portions of the area between the ribs of the pumpkin. These short, perhaps only 1"-2", slits can open deep cuts into the pumpkin, eventually exposing the seed cavity to air. Fortunately, the stem-end of the pumpkin has the thickest walls, so a stem split does not have to signal the end of your pumpkin. The first line of defense is an application of a fungicide, in paste form, to form a poultice over the split.

Note the circular ring that travels from side-to-side across the blossom end of John Castellucci's 682.4-pound, 1996 Rhode Island state record pumpkin. This is a good example of a Dill ring on a beautiful Atlantic Giant.

Pasting with a Fungicide

This technique is fairly common among competitive pumpkin growers. Using either Captan or Benlate (Benomyl), first place a few tablespoons of the fungicide into a small container, mixing a small amount of water to the wettable powder to make a thick slurry. Only a small amount of water is needed. You want this mix to have the consistency of thick paint because, you will, indeed, be applying it to the pumpkin like paint. Using a 1", soft-bristled paint brush, dab the mixture into the splits around and on the stem. Also use it to paint over small cracks that occur in the skin of the pumpkin, along with any injuries the pumpkin sustains from mishandling or varmint invasions. Anytime you have areas of the fruit that are weeping, this paste should be used to prevent disease from entering the pumpkin, and to dry-out the area as quickly as possible. You should apply the paste once-a-week, building-up over previous applications to insure that the splits thoroughly dry and harden. I prefer to use Benlate because I have found that Captan has a tendency to dry and flake-off as new applications are applied, but both work marvelously at drying cracks and splits and preventing diseases from gaining a foothold.

At the end of the season, you will have to remove the fungicide from the pumpkin because many weigh off sites will not allow pumpkins to compete with it still present. This is a good idea because children are bound to be touching your pumpkin, and these fungicides are not intended

This cross section of John Castellucci's 1996, 682.4-pound pumpkin shows an angular internal crack which never fully surfaced. Note that the wall thickness at this point is less than half the thickness of the surrounding walls, and a mere fraction of the thickness of the thickest parts of the pumpkin's walls.

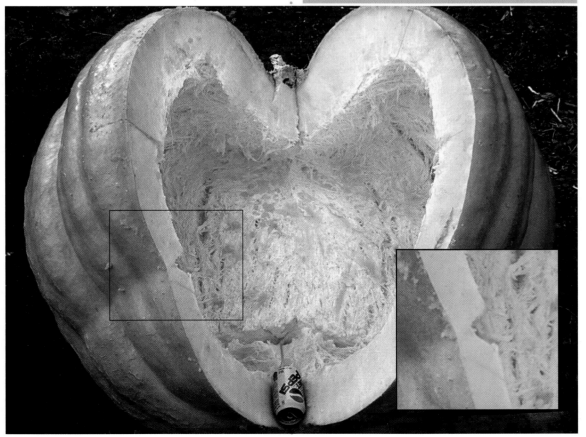

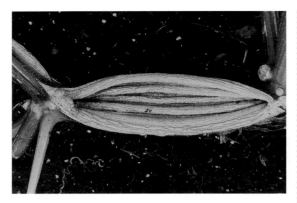

for hand to mouth contacts. A little bleach and water along with a soft brush can easily remove any buildup on the fruit and restore the beauty of your specimen.

Get your pumpkin into exhibition condition by cleaning it with bleach and water just prior to the weigh off, and then give it a soft rub-down with a furniture polish, like *Lemon Pledge,* or an application of *WiltPruf* (an antitranspirant). They will reduce moisture loss while creating a lustrous finish to the skin.

Stem splits and Dill rings are but a few of the many things that can, and will, go wrong if you have a competitive pumpkin going into late August, early September. Sometimes avoidance is not possible. Most times, you can only reduce the stresses exerted by these forces. Repositioning the pumpkin can alleviate some stem stress, but you do it at the risk of injuring the fruit, or ending the season in an instant. Some growers have used bungy cords and weights to counterbalance some of the force exerted on the stem by the vine. It will take a few years of experience and a good eye to know which course of action will be best for your particular pumpkin. For now, network with other experienced growers, get their opinions and rely on a wealth of knowledge and experience that is available to any serious giant pumpkin grower who wants to learn.

Mutant Plants

I have seen a lot of strange things occurring over the last few years, and my only explanation is that *Atlantic Giants* have become so closely pollinated

Top left: A vine may split apart, but this problem, in most cases, causes no ill effects on the plant.
Above: Jack LaRue examines damage caused from hailstones in June. This is one of those rare occasions when a freak thunderstorm did not end the season for a grower – an exception to Murphy's Law.

to itself that rare mutations are beginning to show at much higher rates. The most common of these is multiple vines connected to one another in a fashion that presents the vine as a thick ribbon composed of several vines, each complete with their own tendrils, male and female flowers and side vines. I have had double and triple vines myself, and I have observed other growers with as many as 5-6 vines all attached to one another. I have yet to see anyone set multiple fruit and grow them out with any success. After battling a couple of plants over two seasons, I decided that it was wiser to prune the multiple vine off, and concentrate on other singular vines on the same plant as candidates for fruit set. My good friend, Tim Donovan of Norton, MA, did just that in 1997 and ended up

with a 676-pound pumpkin on a side vine that came off of his deadheaded, multiple vine. In the long run, I believe that early detection and pruning of a multiple vine will reduce the work you have to do later, and improve your chances of producing a competitive pumpkin on the plant.

Another strange occurrence, but happening more frequently, is female flowers with more than one pumpkin attached to their base. I call these Siamese twins because of the way that the fruit are connected to one another and share the same flower as their means of pollination. Usually these Siamese twins will have 8-12 female stamens (segments or lobes) inside the flower. One could theorize that if 5 segments is better than 4 segments, then, perhaps, 12 segments is better still. I have never heard of anyone growing one of these mutants up to competitive size.

The question of whether to spend time with one of these rarities is up to you. I would guess that anyone who has the opportunity to grow one of these has the responsibility to do so. You can certainly dream about a pumpkin that could be double the weight of anything else grown on that plant. If you think that way, the enthusiasm and interest of growing that particular pumpkin could create a very memorable season. Until someone grows a big one from one of these Siamese twins, you will have to be cognizant of the fact that you will be growing a pumpkin that has a high probability of producing less than competitive specimens.

Top right: A Siamese Twin pumpkin – No one has yet to grow one of these mutants to a world class weight.
Above left: An attempt to keep a badly cracked stem dry by directing air from a small fan onto it.
Left: A 13-segment flower is as rare as a royal, straight flush, and just as likely to produce a large fruit.

chapter fifteen

Late Protection

Keeping your plant and pumpkin healthy through September could mean the difference between squeezing-out those last few pounds or finishing second to your next-door neighbor

ate protection is a matter of personal choice, although pumpkins with a reasonable chance at bettering your personal best, or breaking a local or regional record, or establishing a new world record, should be given serious attention before the expected first frost date. September is not a month that is synonymous with tremendous pumpkin growth, but squeezing 100 pounds or more from this month can mean the difference between personal satisfaction or despair at not having given a maximum effort. Any grower wishing to maximize the growth of his pumpkin should provide some late protection.

Late protection can be as simple as placing a blanket and tarp over your pumpkin on cold evenings to keep it warm and dry, or as complete as providing a greenhouse environment created through the use of plastic or Remay row covering. Your pumpkin's prospects, along with your interest and enthusiasm, will determine if the added time, work and expenses is warranted.

James Kuhn of New Hampshire checks late season protection for his 1997, 929.4 pound pumpkin. Keeping the fruit warm and dry in September has proven to aid greatly in improving growth and condition.

Above: A protective fence with a covering of plastic creates a microclimate that prevents hard frosts from occurring all through the month of September.

well below freezing. At most, this structure will be up for 3-4 weeks, but the benefits are continued growth of the fruit, and an environment that is more conducive to holding your specimen until weigh off day.

Some growers cover their entire plant, suspending the covering above the plant using barrels, wire or anything available. Sides are buried in the soil to hold it down in the wind, and unburied on extremely warm days to prevent over heating of the space. Creating large structures with pvc pipe, much the same as the Emmons' early greenhouses (presented in *Chapter 1, Heavy Hitters*) provides structures that can be used at both ends of the season with amazing effectiveness. Portable space heaters can be fired up on nights when temperatures are expected to go

Keeping Your Pumpkin Dry

It is important to keep your pumpkin dry at all times at the close of the season. Shade protection that was properly erected earlier in the season will usually form the basis for achieving this objective, but cool, moist September days and nights can present additional problems. The leaf canopy of the plant is now quite full and air circulation is not as good as it was earlier in the season. Trimming some leaves in the vicinity of the fruit will allow for better air movement, and consequently faster and better drying. If your fruit has splits and scars that are oozing, keep these areas as dry as possible and continuously coated with a fungicide paste like Captan or Benlate, and provide additional air circulation. Some growers will direct small portable fans at vulnerable areas of the fruit to insure that dry conditions are maintained.

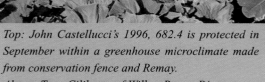

Top: John Castellucci's 1996, 682.4 is protected in September within a greenhouse microclimate made from conservation fence and Remay.
Above: Tony Ciliberto of Wilkes-Barre, PA creates a structure that keeps the fruit from being exposed to cold September nights.

Keeping Your Pumpkin's Exterior Free from Disease

A once-a-week application of bleach and water (10 parts water to 1 part bleach) to the fruit during September will insure that spores and any surface diseases are eliminated. This can be applied with a small spray bottle or with a soft, cloth soaked in the solution. *ZeroTolerance,* a horticultural disinfectant, can be used in place of common, household bleach. Anti dessicants and antitranspirant sprays like *WiltPruf* can also be used to prevent any loss of moisture from the fruit. Remember, 80% of the weight of a pumpkin comes from the water it holds in its cells. It is also advised that you include seaweed extracts in your fertilizing program during the growing season. Seaweed has been proven to improve the shelf life of vegetables and fruits, and the benefit to a pumpkin grower is the reduced likelihood of rotting or premature ripening.

Above: Glen Brown's late season protection keeps the entire plant and fruit free from damaging weather. Below: Kirk Mombert's plant gets the royal treatment with this Remay and plastic enclosure.

Protecting Your Pumpkin From Invaders

Critters like woodchucks, possum, and raccoons will occasionally lunch on maturing pumpkins. They generally do not consume much, but their teeth and claw marks can destroy the overall beauty of the fruit, and allow for easier access of disease. A barricade can be erected around the fruit to prevent these invasions, but special care must be made to prevent damage to the plant and fruit during its construction. Some growers use 4' x 4' pallets, held up with steel posts, to completely enclose the pumpkin. This prevents large critters from getting to the fruit, and at the same time, provides reasonable air circulation. It also keeps your friends and neighbors from getting too close to your prized pumpkin.

chapter sixteen

Competing and Having Fun!

Finding out how big your pumpkin is, and how you stack-up against your fellow pumpkin growers is a joy that cannot be overlooked. At every weigh off you'll meet new people and make new friends for life.

For many, the joy of growing a giant pumpkin would not be complete without an end of season competition to garner recognition, measure one's self against other growers, to meet old friends again, and to share the joy that all big pumpkins bring. In recent years, these events have exploded in both number and importance to growers. Prizes have escalated to thousands of dollars for some of the premier weigh offs, while simple ribbons and trophies satisfy the bulk of competitors at the smaller events. Scheduling where you compete can be almost as difficult a question as how you grow your pumpkin, because on any given weekend in September and October, there is likely to be a multitude of options on where you can go with your giant pumpkin. Obviously, the first Saturday in October should be reserved for competing at one of the sanctioned events staged by either the

Phill Simpson of Solana Beach, CA had no alternative for removing his giant pumpkin from his backyard. Unable to get his pumpkin between the closely constructed homes, his friend brought in a crane, and took his giant over the house.

Above: Al Eaton hoists his '97, 853-pound pumpkin from the garden with homemade block and tackle.

Above: John Castellucci of Smithfield, RI lifts his 1997, 743-pound pumpkin — or is that an alligator? Below: Geneva Emmons', 1996, 939-pounder is raised by a timber, boom truck

GPC, WPC, IPA or a large independent site with high exposure to pumpkin growers. This Saturday will produce news on the biggest pumpkin grown in the world for any given year, and bringing a larger pumpkin to a weigh off before or after this date is likely to be discounted by competitive pumpkin growers, the media, and the record keeping bodies.

I generally start competing in mid-August at local fairs using culled fruit that are far from being my heaviest. 400-500-pound pumpkins will generally win these early weigh offs and send shock waves through the pumpkin growing community as to who has got what. You will see the same people at these early, smaller weigh offs as you will see at the big, end-of-season events, so its a nice time to rekindle friendships that you've made over the years, and to begin what I call the "chess match." I call it a chess match because these early weigh offs can

be a time of great speculation as to who has what in your area. I find this curiosity and suspense to be one of the more enjoyable parts of the sport. "If he has a 500-pounder now, what is he likely to

Above: Ron and Dick Wallace's 1997, 628-pound pumpkin is hand-loaded by five growers.
Bottom left: Don Langevin and Steve Connolly proudly pose after traveling 750 miles to the Raleigh, NC State Farmers' Market Weigh Off.
Bottom right: A Jack LaRue pumpkin is placed in a pickup with paneled sides to keep wind from accelerating the loss of water that inevitably occurs once the fruit is cut from the vine.

have at home?" Many growers bring a low-key attitude to these early events, not wishing to reveal what they actually have at home, and not wishing to be exposed to the curiosity of other growers. Many purposely paint a picture of a poor growing year, not wanting any additional pressure on themselves to bring a really big one to the end-of-season events. As you will see, most experienced growers know that anything can happen, at any time; and unbridled enthusiasm can sometimes create real disappointment in the end. So, to get a true picture of what is going on, you have to go to the big, end-of-season weigh offs in your area, and earlier in the season, you'll just have to guess and play the chess match.

Besides finding these events, you should be aware of a number of other small questions that all growers should know the answers to before they decide to compete anywhere. How you get your pumpkin from your patch to the competition, how you get your pumpkin from your vehicle to the event staging area and what the rules will be, are but a few of these small questions.

Loading and Unloading

I did not cover this subject in my first book, but have since determined that it is one of the most frequently asked questions by new growers. Even the biggest pumpkin in the world can be moved by hand, provided you have enough of them. Any pumpkin can be successfully moved and loaded without damage to fruit or man, if it is done thoughtfully. I would say that it will take a minimum of one strong person per hundred pounds of estimated weight to move a giant (more than that will make the task easier). Twelve people moved Craig Weir's, 1994, 914 off the trailer it arrived in to the staging area — all had red faces and white knuckles when it was done. 500-pound pumpkins can safely be loaded with the assistance of five or six people. I do not want you to assume that this is an easy task. The loading and unloading of a giant pumpkin should be treated with concern. People can get hurt if a pumpkin's weight exceeds their strength.

The pumpkin should be hoisted using a large tarpaulin. Many growers use specially made pumpkin carriers that have handles for a dozen or more men to hold onto. Using an inexpensive plastic tarp will do the trick, but someone is likely to get skinned knuckles if the pumpkin is particularly heavy, and the likelihood of dropping and damaging the pumpkin are much higher. The hand-made pumpkin carriers will average between $60-$100 depending on size. A 4'x4' carrier can be used to lift up to 500 pounds, a 5'x5' up to 800 pounds and a 6'x6' for anything heavier.

Moving a giant pumpkin should be taken in steps. First, roll the pumpkin up onto its side. Do not roll it onto its stem or blossom end. Once up, it can be easily balanced while someone places a tarp beneath the fruit. Let the pumpkin down carefully, and then roll it onto its other side. Pull the tarp under so that the pumpkin is centered on the tarp. If it is not centered, a disproportionate amount of weight will be carried by a few lifters. Centering the fruit will distribute the weight equally to all lifters. Working as a team, lift and carry the pumpkin to the rear of your pickup (or other vehicle). Set it down and plan the most difficult part of loading – getting the pumpkin from the ground to a pallet in the bed of your truck. At least two people should be standing in the truck bed. While others lift from the ground, the two in the bed pull up and into the truck (being careful to clear the truck body and pallet). Once in the truck, several people should reposition the fruit for optimum stability. Having padding on the pallet should go without saying. If you are travelling hundreds of miles to a weigh off, the fruit should be covered with a tarp, and the tarp should be securely fastened to the pallet or truck body. Check out what Joel Holland does in *Chapter 1, The Heavy Hitters*.

You should know in advance how your weigh off plans to remove your pumpkin from your vehicle. Some now use fork trucks which makes it imperative that you load your pumpkin onto a pallet with the pallet positioned properly to receive the forks of the truck. Most weigh offs still use designated

Above and to right: Roll pumpkin on side-rib, slide tarp under; roll to other side, pull tarp flat; lift. Almost all giant pumpkin growers do it this way, even with pumpkins weighing 1000 pounds!

Below: If you have the equipment – use it, but the delicate removal of the pumpkin from the patch will still take some help from strong men regardless of the equipment you plan on using.

Rules

Rules and regulations may vary from site to site and organization to organization, but there are some general rules followed by most weigh offs that inject some consistency into the weighing of giant pumpkins. The WPC and GPC have done a good job in fostering guidelines which allow for some flexibility yet provides a just and fair framework in which all growers can compete. Some of the basic rules you are likely to encounter are:

lifting teams, and the assistance of the grower and his family and friends to unload, weigh and load all pumpkins. Be prepared to help others at these smaller events.

An exhibitor (husband and wife as one) may enter only one specimen per class (pumpkin or squash).

An exhibitor must be present for the competition. (You cannot just drop your pumpkin off).

To be declared a pumpkin, the fruit must be cream-yellow to orange in color.

A specimen must be healthy and undamaged and free from holes that penetrate to the interior. Vines will be trimmed to one inch from stem. Foreign material may not be included in the weighing.

When you are totally stumped as to how you will move your giant, take a look at page 126 and what Phill Simpson conjured when he found that his pumpkin would not fit between the tightly clustered homes of his neighborhood in southern California — bring in the crane!

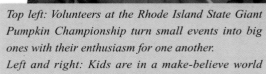

Top left: Volunteers at the Rhode Island State Giant Pumpkin Championship turn small events into big ones with their enthusiasm for one another.
Left and right: Kids are in a make-believe world anytime they are around a giant pumpkin.

The winning pumpkin will be judged by weight alone. Circumference, shape or general appearance have no bearing on the competition unless a prize sponsor has designated that its prize money will go to the most beautiful, largest in circumference, etc.

Etiquette

The golden rule certainly applies here – "Treat others as you would have them treat you." You will be immensely proud of your entry, and so will everyone else at the event. Growers that have coddled their pumpkins for three months are not likely to want others handling or touching them (with the exception of helping them to load and unload). I discourage anyone who competes from touching a fellow competitor's pumpkin. Too often, I have seen unintended damage produced from curious onlookers who must touch a giant pumpkin to prove to themselves that it is real. A giant pumpkin displayed for just one day in a high traffic area will have hundreds of fingernail marks to mark the curiosity of people. Try to keep your children under control at these events. Kids will be particularly pumped-up in the presence of these giants. Left to their own, they will climb the specimens like giant boulders and ride them with the spurs kicking. I love kids, so this is an opportune time for parents to teach their children the importance of respecting what others hold dear. Help one another and make as many friends as you can on these rare days that combine competition and camaraderie. Friends you make at these weigh offs will be friends for the rest of your life.

Above: Vern Lawrence, Jack LaRue, Dale Montague and Lincoln Mettler remove seeds from the pumpkins they displayed in 1997 at Remlinger Farms in Carnation, WA.

Sportsmanship

Being a good sport should be the hallmark of each and every weigh off you attend. Win, place or show, be friendly, gracious and thankful. Know the rules in advance and abide by them. If you have any questions concerning the eligibility of your fruit, don't bring it to a weigh off. Life is too short to be labeled as an opportunist that would try to benefit from bending the rules. If it's a squash — it's a squash! If it has a hole in it that goes right through, don't patch it and see if it can get by, disqualify the pumpkin yourself at home, and bring something else to the weigh off. Above all, respect your fellow growers.

This page shows two pictures of giant squash. These are green, but they can also be gray with yellow and orange also present. The rule for pumpkins states that the fruit must be predominantly cream yellow to orange. 75% to 80% is most often used for rulings.
To the right: Joel Holland props his granddaughter, Taylor, atop the 1997, 879. I don't know who's happier — Joel or Taylor.

chapter seventeen

What do you do with that?

Invariably, someone will ask you, "What do you do with your giant pumpkin at the end of the season?" There are, surprisingly, many things to do — some obvious, some rather bizarre!

Get ready to answer round after round of the same set of questions. "Is that real?" "Did you feed it milk?" "How long did that take you to grow?" And, "What do you do with that now?"

The obvious use is pumpkin pies, but I have yet to taste a pumpkin pie made from an *Atlantic Giant.* "Too much work," says my wife, Anne — "and besides, a can of prepared pumpkin cost just 79¢ at the supermarket." You can make pies and other goodies using your favorite recipes, but add a bit more sugar (these aren't sugar pumpkins) and experiment with your favorite seasonings and spices.

To left: Joel Holland's sculpted, 1997, 879-pound pumpkin. This is the same pumpkin that appears on page 135.

Above: Janet and Gary Keyzer, and their children, of Nekoosa, WI are intense giant pumpkin growers and equally intense carvers. Only Christmas outshines the joy they get from the Halloween season.

Also remember the amount of pesticide spraying you did and when. Perhaps it is better to use this monster pumpkin as a decoration, and forego the consumption of insecticides and fungicides.

Above: Julie Langevin, daughter of the author, with an Elliott Lewin III sculpture in 1994.
Below: Dry ice and creative lighting can make for a dramatic display as was done with this Joel Holland, 1997, 879-pounder.

Painting

Painting pumpkins has become quite popular among early age children because of the relative ease (compared to carving) and the introduction of child safe paints that can be easily cleaned-up after. At the RI Giant Pumpkin Championship, we set up a pumpkin painting area complete with child-sized tables and chairs, non-toxic, non-stain paint, small sugar pumpkins and adult supervision. This is one of the

liveliest areas all through the weigh off day. Painting pumpkins is a very creative alternative to carving, and in many instances, the results are just as satisfying. Check out page 137 to see what Gary Keyzer's family does every Halloween. In some cases, painting is combined with carving to add a new dimension to jack o'lantern displays. Paints can be purchased at any craft or hobby store.

Carving

Carving a giant pumpkin, even one weighing 400-800 pounds, can be a lot simpler than you think. The same procedures you used as a child in carving jack-o'lanterns for Halloween still apply — just the tools have changed. Instead of a small kitchen knife, you'll be using a pruning saw with course-cutting teeth. It will saw right through 10 inches of wall with ease. You can use your favorite vegetable peeling knife to do most of the fine tuning. Carving a giant should take no more than an hour (not including the time it takes to retrieve seeds from the interior). If you want to get elaborate with your giant pumpkin, the next level in creative pumpkin carving is sculpting.

Sculpting

Over the years I have seen many sculpted giant pumpkins. They never stop amazing me with their ghoulish features and intricately sculpted flesh. The basic difference between carving and sculpting is the use of various depths of cut to produce 3-dimensional features. When carving, you cut holes that create two levels of light (light and dark). The holes you cut emit light from the interior of the pumpkin, accenting the shapes of

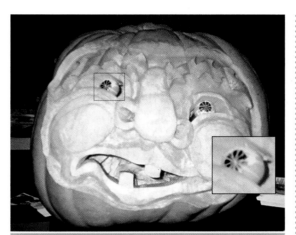

Above: An Elliott Lewin, Jr. creation for a local mall. Notice the small gourds used for eyes.

the eyes, nose and mouth. When sculpting, you create many levels of light. You still have light and dark, but you also have the translucent light that permeates through all areas of the pumpkin's face that are sculpted to various depths. Eyebrows and the tip of the nose might be left entirely alone, while areas around the nose, mouth and eyes are deeply sculpted — producing many levels of light that accent these areas, as well as the areas they abut.

Perhaps the master of pumpkin sculptors is Sam Gendusa from Dayton, Oregon (King of the Punkin Carvers). Sam's book, *Carving Jack-O'-Lanterns,* is a very complete treatment of carving and preparing your pumpkin for exhibition, as well as giving a good history of this tradition. From this book, you can learn in detail many of the things that we cover in the next few paragraphs.

Tools

You will need a felt-tipped marker to draw a face onto the pumpkin. It helps to have an idea of what you want your jack-o-lantern to look like when it's finished, before you start to cut into it. You will need a large serrated knife or pruning saw to cut the large areas out, which include the eye openings, nostrils and mouth. You can also use the saw to cut an opening in the rear of the pumpkin, or to cut the top off, so you can retrieve the seeds.

Other tools include a 3/4" wood gouge (a sculptor's tool) and a small wooden mallet for roughly sculpting the areas around the eyes, nose and mouth. A vegetable peeler is used to further fine-tune areas and to smooth the finish of the completed jack-o-lantern. A small paring knife can be used to cleanup sharp details that the other tools cannot achieve. Many amateur pumpkin sculptors create their own tools from an assortment of kitchen utensils.

According to Gendusa "There are four procedures in carving a creative jack-o-lantern: (1) design, (2) cut, (3) carve and (4) finish." Design and layout your creation on paper first, then transfer it to the pumpkin's face. Cut-out the larger areas first. Always work from large to small cuts using progressively smaller tools as you go along. After the large holes are cut, the carving procedure begins. Use the hammer and gouge to rough-out your design. When you can go no further with these tools, switch to the vegetable peeler to excavate the remaining areas and to finish your jack-o-

Above: Del Edwards of Smithfield, RI sits inside John Castellucci's, 1996, 682.4-pound pumpkin with her treasured cat, Freckles.

Above: Sherry LaRue's 1997, 1016 makes a dramatic sculpture. Sculpted by: Pam Burns and Russ Leno.

pumpkin. They can be held in place with round toothpicks. (Note the fashioned eyes in the photos to the left and right and on the previous page.)

Sculpting, even the most elaborate design, should take no more than four hours. Your creation is highly perishable and will last no more than a week if not protected. A number of products can be used to extend the life of the sculpture including spray fixatives (used by artists to protect drawings), furniture polish (like Lemon Pledge) or Wilt Pruf (an antitranspirant, anti-dessicant that is safe to use on all types of plant material).

lantern. Use the serrated side first, then go back later to smooth-out the marks with the flat side of the peeler. Now the paring knife can be used to sharpen details that the other tools cannot achieve. Eyes can be fashioned from small gourds, other vegetables or pieces of the excavated flesh of the

After completing your carved jack-o-lantern there are some tricks for getting the most out of its display. Since a candle does not have sufficient light to show-off a giant pumpkin, electric light should be used. Suspend a 20-60 watt red light bulb inside, right behind the nose. You can use one of those extensions that has a caged bulb-fixture on

Below: Mari Lou and Joel Holland with their grandson, Jacob, at Disneyland in 1995.

the end (the type mechanics use to light the interior of an engine compartment). For exterior lighting use colored spot lights, or put colored screens in front of flood lights. If you have the desire, cut an opening in the back that is large enough to place an electric hot plate inside. Use this to heat a pan of water into which dry ice can be emersed. The billowing smoke it will produce can be channeled through the nostrils by covering the interior openings of the eyes and mouth with clear plastic wrap. The red interior light, and the colored flood lights will paint a picture you will long remember.

Above: Geneva Emmons' 1997, 556-pound pumpkin sculpted by Sleepy Hollow.
Left: Elliott Lewin sculpts a pumpkin at the weigh off for the Rhode Island State Giant Pumpkin Championship.
Below: Sculptures from the Clackamas, OR weigh off.

So now we've looked at a few obvious uses for a giant pumpkin, besides competing for family, neighborhood or local bragging rights. Considering the bizarre size of these giants, it's only fitting that they should also have a bizarre use as well. Would you believe pumpkin boat races?

Boating

He may not be the Pumpkin King, but Wayne Hackney of New Milford, CT more than qualifies as the Pumpkin Pirate. Wayne single handedly navigated a two-mile crossing of a lake in Connecticut in 1996, on rough seas, to claim the distinction of being the first to use a giant pumpkin as a boat. His "Mighty Mabel" was equipped with an outboard motor and managed a barge-like 2 miles per hour. This singular act in November of 1996 sparked the interest of a number of grower/yachtsmen who planned and ran a race in New York's Central Park in October of 1997. Three pumpkins chugged their way around waters lined with media folk and spectators — all of which stood with awe-struck expressions as grown men behaved as children. This really is what giant pumpkin growing is all about. Not the boating, mind you, but the return of men and women to childhood pursuits. Pumpkin growing is supposed to be fun. Hackney and others in the sport serve to constantly remind us that life really is too short, and once in a while, even mature men must clown around.

Exhibiting

After the weigh offs are concluded, you may want to exhibit your pumpkin in a public place. Doing this will obviously garner you additional recognition for your achievement, but this will come at the expense of exposing your pumpkin to curious onlookers that cannot thwart their temptation to touch your pumpkin. I recommend that you plan on displaying your pumpkin in such a manner that it is elevated off the ground approximately 4' and corralled with a rope fence to keep spectators 4'-5' away. This will reduce damage. Elevating it will insure that everyone has a good view of it, and corralling it insures that it will not be touched. If it is to be displayed outside, have someone bring it in at night, or at times when security is not provided. A giant pumpkin is a huge temptation for pranksters bent on the ultimate pumpkin smashing.

Selling

Giant pumpkins have become very popular display items over the last several years. In my first book I offered a guideline for selling giants based on my observations at the time, but what I have learned since judges those recommendations as grossly understated. An average jack o'lantern sized pumpkin sells for anywhere between 25¢ and 39¢ a pound depending on your location and the crop yield for the year. Giant pumpkins command a lot more because they are used generally by commercial establishments to create memorable displays for their customers. As a result, the value of giants as promotional props escalates their value. Banks, grocery stores, garden centers, indoor malls, casinos and amusement parks, and on and on, see giant pumpkins as a reasonable expense in a marketing and promotion budget that

The three competitors churned up a lake in Central Park, followed by Jeannie Most and a film crew from CNN Headline News.

is weighted with very costly newspaper, radio and TV ad purchases. An outstanding specimen, (good shape, color and condition) that weighs more than 500 pounds, is very saleable. Of course, you have to go out and find the people that would be willing to pay good money for your pumpkin, but I assure you, they are out there.

If your pumpkin has won a significant, local, regional or national weigh off, this will serve to

further raise its fair value. The largest pumpkin in a town, state, region, country or the world will all serve to promote additional interest in it which will benefit the purchaser of the specimen.

Professional pumpkin carvers will also be looking for outstanding specimens to sculpture and sell to their clients, although they may not be willing to pay as much for your fruit as you would be able to secure for it in the open market. Businessmen,

On this page we see a pumpkin opened up for retrieval of seeds and then sculpted for exhibition. Notice that the blossom end is removed instead of the stem end, and a tracing is applied before any carving starts.

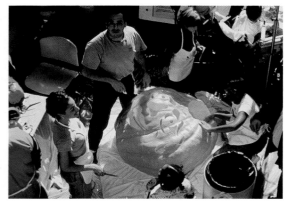

Above: A classic fall picture of, "In search of the perfect jack o'lantern."
Below: Al Berard has some fun with a misshapened, Atlantic Giant pumpkin.

with an eye for creating a dramatic event, may buy your pumpkin merely for the use of it in a giant, pumpkin smashing. This is good clean fun that may satisfy the universal desire of some young teenage boys to smash their neighbor's pumpkin in the middle of the street (although this has never been proven). The more contacts you make with people, and the more you spread the idea of selling your pumpkin, the more likely you will be of receiving a fair price for it. As an update to my first book published in 1993, I offer the following guidelines for selling your giant pumpkin:

300-499	40¢/lb.	$120-$200
500-699	50¢/lb.	$250-$350
700-899	$1/lb.	$700-900
900-999	$4/lb.	$3600-4000
1000+	$10/lb.	$10,000+

Add 10% to the above prices for good shape, color, condition or a notable achievement. Deduct 20% for poor color or shape or a defect.

Sharing the Joy

If you have ever stood back and observed people when they are looking at a pumpkin (any pumpkin, but particularly a giant or carved one), you will inevitably see people with smiles on their faces. It is universal. No matter what age, sex or race, a pumpkin has an effect on everyone which brings with it an instant of goodness and joy. Children are particularly bewitched by pumpkins and there is a little bit of the child in each and every one of us. Giant pumpkin growers, therefore, bask in an aura that pumpkins produce anyplace where people and giant pumpkins are present. Ask pumpkin growers why they drive around town, for sometimes more than a month after a weigh off, with a giant pumpkin in the back of their pickup truck. They become everyone's friend as passing motorists signal an approving "thumbs-up" and every parking lot is an opportunity for people to congregate around you.

Knowing this, many growers have unselfishly taken their precious time to expose their giants to children that otherwise would not have had the opportunity. One individual that I particularly admire, John Castellucci of Smithfield, RI, takes his largest pumpkin each year to the Hasbro Children's Hospital in Providence, RI. You would have to see the looks on these tiny faces who are, in many cases, terminally ill to know that a pumpkin can work miracles in the minds of God's little people. John is but one of many growers who annually spreads the joy of pumpkins and shares his love of the sport with those who are less fortunate. If you need a lift, try giving a little back to the sport of pumpkin growing by finding ways for other people to see what you have grown. You will be doing them a great service — and yourself as well.

Saving Seeds

Saving seeds from the giant pumpkin you grew is a fairly easy task, and you will want to save some of them because friends and acquaintances will ask for them when they see how big your pumpkin is. This is a good way to introduce someone to the sport, and to share the joy of growing giant pumpkins. Properly retrieving, cleaning, drying and storing will insure that you have more than enough seeds to distribute to your friends.

Any pumpkin that grows out to full maturity will have a large number of seeds. The average pumpkin will have between 400-600 seeds, although this can vary considerably depending on pollination and state of maturity at harvest. The longer you leave a pumpkin on the vine, the higher the probability that seeds inside will be fully developed with reliable germination.

If you are planning to carve or sculpture your pumpkin, seed retrieval will be an easy task that adds little to the total time of creating a jack o'lantern. Many will retrieve their seeds by cutting an opening in the rear or bottom of the pumpkin that is less conspicuous than cutting off the top (stem end). A hole that is approximately 12"-15" in diameter should give you ample maneuvering space to reach in and search for seeds.

Once seeds are retrieved, wash them thoroughly with clean, running water. Try to wash away as much pulp as possible. The seeds will have a slimy feel to them, but this coating will eventually dry and flake off of the seed. The key to preserving seeds is to get them dried as quickly as possible. Freshly harvested seed are high in moisture content, and this moisture can contribute to rotting, or premature germination if left to persist for too long a period under warm temperature conditions. Also, adequate air circulation must be provided to accelerate evaporation of this moisture. I have found that temperatures above 80 degrees work best.

I first place newly washed seeds onto dry newspaper, creating a single layer of seed. The moisture present from washing will soak the paper, so after 24 hours, discard this paper and use fresh, dry newspaper. Place the seeds in a warm place that gets good air circulation. I put my seeds near a wood stove where temperatures are very warm.

After 1-2 weeks of drying, you will begin to notice that a membrane (almost like very thin plastic) will begin to flake from the exterior of the seed. This is a sure sign that the seed has begun to dry, and not much more time will be required to insure that the seed is left in a state that will allow it to store for many years with very good germination percentages.

The total time to prepare seeds for storage should be approximately three weeks. After the drying process, place your seeds in containers which will allow them to breathe. Paper bags, or jars with holes in the lid will provide just enough air to keep the seed adjusted to its new home without deterioration. Some growers will also dust their seeds with a fungicide, like *Captan,* to insure that diseases are kept in check.

If you carefully retrieve fully developed seeds, dry them properly, and store them under good conditions, you should be able to enjoy the fruits of your labor for many, many years. Pumpkin seeds will germinate many years after harvest. Seeds that are 4-6 years old are routinely germinated each year, and it remains to be seen, just how long you can store and successfully germinate them.

Below: Growers at the Remlinger Farm, Carnation, WA weigh off site end their season by taking seeds from the giants they have grown, and returning the balance to the compost pile.

chapter eighteen

World Class Sites & Associations

When growing a giant pumpkin, a lot of the fun comes from competing and associating with other growers, and many associations publish quarterly newsletters to keep their members on the cutting edge of the sport.

I cannot stress enough the need for anyone interested in improving as a giant pumpkin grower to network with other growers, both locally and internationally. This is easier than it appears because most, competitive giant pumpkin growers enjoy helping other growers, sharing ideas and seeds and generally partaking in the fraternity of the sport. Most are members in several associations or grower groups. The key way to find out who it is in your area that is experienced, or find out who is experiencing success, is to join associations or organizations that are created for people in the sport – there are a number of them. Most of these associations publish periodic newsletters that keep their members abreast of what is going on in their area and in the world of giant pumpkins. Since most of these memberships are nominally priced ($10-$20 per year), I highly encourage everyone to join a local or regional association, and also a successful association in another part of the world.

Nothing is more joyful for children than to experience a pumpkin, and nothing is more satisfying to a competitive pumpkin grower than associating with others that share his interests.

Above: Gus Saunders, affectionately known as Farmer Gus, has been a driving force behind the elevated exposure of the sport to new growers, media and commercial sponsorship. He is the director of the Ottawa-St. Lawrence Growers Association.

149

I encourage you to compete at as many good weigh offs as possible, because it is here that the cream of the crop in growing giant pumpkins will congregate on an annual basis. You will see the same faces at many of these weigh offs and this becomes a perfect opportunity to meet good growers and develop friendships that will last for many, many years. Networking with these growers, and joining their

A list of associations and sites appears in the appendix of this book, and we will highlight some of the more successful ones in the following pages.

Ottawa-St. Lawrence Growers

This organization, headed-up by "Farmer Gus" Saunders, has come from nowhere in 1991 to one of the premier associations and weigh offs in the world. Their top-ten average weights has dominated every other site in the world for the past four years, and they were the first association to organize and stage an annual growers' seminar in 1995. They have initiated many new ideas including: seed raffling and seed distribution of world

Top left: the 700 Club annually poses for pictures at the Ottawa-St. Lawrence growers' seminar.
Below: Competitors and volunteers pose for a group picture at Park's Garden Center in Canfield, OH for the Ohio Valley Giant Pumpkin Growers Weigh Off.

class *Atlantic Giant* seed stocks, and development of an interactive web site for distribution of information to anyone interested in growing giant pumpkins. They print a series of cards each year of top growers at their weigh off that are given as momentos to anyone who is a member of their association. They are indeed an

associations will insure that you are always on the cutting edge of news in the sport concerning new cultural methods and new, hot seed stocks.

international organization, boasting more than 500 members from Canada, the United States, Japan and many other countries. Their newsletters, published quarterly, are the very best available, both in content and amount of informa-

tion conveyed. Their weigh off, in the ByWard Market in downtown Ottawa, Ontario, Canada, draws thousands of spectators to an area of the city that is a bustle of people and commerce. Their enthusiastic members, and energized leadership, are a model to all small associations. This large weigh off site is presently a member of the GPC.

Top left: The RI Pumpkin Growers Association stages their annual state championship.
Top right: An informal grower get-together provides for exchange of growing ideas and seeds.
Below: The 1061 is lowered to the scale at the WPC weigh off in Collins, NY in 1996.

New England Pumpkin Growers Association (NEPGA)

Under the ever present eye and management of Hugh Wiberg, this organization, started in 1989, has grown to become one of the strongest in the world. Their quarterly newsletters are informative for the New England growers, but also useful for

Circleville, OH annually stages one of the most exciting harvest festivals in the world. Here, Main Street is completely shut down to allow for display of things related to the fall harvest.

anyone else growing giant pumpkins anywhere in the world. The NEPGA runs the All New England Pumpkin Championship staged annually at the Topsfield Fair in Topsfield, MA. This large agricultural fair draws in excess of 500,000 people yearly to its ten days of events and competitions. The pumpkin weigh off is held on the first day of the fair, with more than 5000 people in attendance, and more than 100 competitors. This weigh off is the highlight of the year for any giant pumpkin grower in New England. Their annual summer picnic and winter dinner have become traditions. This large weigh off site is presently a member of the GPC, and its director, Wiberg, is also a member of the steering committee for the GPC.

Ohio Valley
Giant Pumpkin Growers

Headed up by site coordinator Tim Parks, this weigh off has become one of the premier sites in the GPC. When the weather is favorable, this group of growers can compete with the world's best. The association publishes a quarterly

newsletter that is edited by Alan Gibson. The members of this association are noted for their dedication to growing giant pumpkins, as well as a steadfast search for as much fun as possible at any giant pumpkin sponsored event. If you go to the Ottawa Giant Pumpkin Seminar, you only have to listen for where the most noise is coming from — and you are bound to find the guys from Ohio. This large weigh off site is a member of the GPC.

Pacific Northwest
Growers Association

Newly formed, but from a rich tradition of giant pumpkin competition, this association boasts some of the best, and most consistent giant pumpkin growers in the world. Their annual weigh off is staged in Carnation, WA at Remlinger Farms where the likes of Joel Holland, Jack LaRue and Kirk Mombert compete. This large weigh off site is presently a member of the GPC.

Windsor, Nova Scotia

Run by Danny Dill, son of the Pumpkin King, Howard Dill, Danny has done a commendable job in organizing growers, staging a world class weigh off and writing and publishing an annual newsletter. This, after all, is a person who "lives, and sleeps" giant pumpkins. Besides these responsibilities, Danny runs the family farm and seed business, oversees the operations of the seed museum and guides tours that routinely visit during the fall and summer months. This site was one of the very first organized under the WPC and later the GPC. They are now an independent site which networks with all of the large weigh offs conducting competitions on the first Saturday of October annually.

Port Elgin, Ontario

The Port Elgin Fall Festival, run by Jan Bonhomme, and the Chamber of Commerce of Port Elgin, Canada is one of the most successful festivals involving pumpkins, and all things that are part of the fall. This community effort is run, sponsored and attended by Port Elgin, and neighboring community, residents. This weigh off site perennially weighs many of the top pumpkins in the world. Presently it is an independent weigh off site, with former affiliations with the WPC.

Great Dixon Mayfair Weigh Off

Staged only 6 miles from the former Nut Tree Weigh Off, in Fairfield, CA, Mike Green, continues to oversee the operations. This large weigh off site is presently a member of the GPC.

Half Moon Bay, CA

This large independent site has been capably run for many years, and attracts most of the very best pumpkin growers on the west coast. They weigh off a few weeks after the world weigh offs, and offer growers the opportunity to compete with other pumpkins.

Rhode Island Pumpkin Growers Association (RIPGA)

The Rhode Island Pumpkin Growers Association was formed in 1994 and has gradually enrolled more and more members each year while their average weights have risen to world class status. An independent weigh off site, their annual event is staged a week after the international weigh offs. Their quarterly newsletter is written and published by Don Langevin, and is considered to be one of the most informative newsletters, from a cultural perspective.

The Port Elgin, Ontario, Canada Chamber of Commerce stages one of the premier giant pumpkin weigh offs and fall festivals in the world. A tent protects spectators from chances of poor weather.

Appendix

Here's a list of weigh offs, associations, seed distributors and product manufacturers that can help you grow your biggest giant pumpkin possible.

This appendix is provided as a starting place in the process that you can follow in locating a convenient weigh off site, an association membership or products for use in the patch. It is by no means complete because these pages could never completely document the thousands of small weigh offs and pumpkin festivals that are staged annually in North America or pretend to present all the different products that could be used in the growing of a giant pumpkin, but it is a start. The major weigh offs are listed with their world, association affiliations. Some of the larger independent weigh off sites are also listed, but this list falls far short of the actual number of sites that weigh off significant-sized pumpkins each year. Your best course of action in locating these other, very good independent sites, which can round-off a great month of September and October weigh offs and exhibitions, is to join one of the major associations and network with other growers in your area. Between the associations and your new giant pumpkin growing friends, you will be kept up-to-date on where and when the best weigh offs occur.

Geneva Emmons' 1997, 854 pound pumpkin was sculpted by Russ Leno and Pam Burns of Sleepy Hollow. Specimens like this become the focal point of weigh offs and fall festivals.

There are three main governing associations that sponsor annual, international weigh offs, and this is constantly being modified, refined or entirely changed. Right now the most successful associations are the GPC (Great Pumpkin Commonwealth) the IPA (International Pumpkin Association) and the WPC (World Pumpkin Confederation). All stage annual weigh offs and coordinate the results from several sites that they oversee. Among them, news of the largest pumpkins grown in the world will be conveyed to the media and through an extremely effective pumpkin grapevine (or should I just simply say pumpkin vine). Each association has leadership that is extremely effective in generating interest from the media and in getting the facts of their weigh offs released to the general public.

The product manufacturers listed are ones that I have personally used, like, and therefore, highly endorse. There are hundreds of other suppliers that could possibly fill your needs. The ones listed here are tried and true, and accustomed to working with competitive giant pumpkin growers.

Weigh Off Sites

GPC (Great Pumpkin Commonwealth) USA

Pennsylvania Pumpkin Bowl
Marvin Meisner, M.D.
Blair Medical Assoc.
1414 Eighth Ave.,
Altoona, PA 16602
(814) 695-7010

Long Island Weigh Off
Andrew Sabin
300 Pantigo Place, Suite 102
East Hampton, NY 11937
(516) 329-1717

Mid-West Pumpkin Growers
Greg & Nancy Norlin
PO Box 195
Anamosa, IA, 52205
(319) 462-4674

Ohio Valley Giant Pumpkin Growers
Tim Parks
9725 W. Calla Road
Salem, OH 44460
(330) 533-7278

Pacific Northwest Giant Pumpkin Growers
Joel Holland
P.O. Box 969
Sumner, WA 98390
(253) 840-3575

Great Illinois Weigh Off
Paul Siegel
Cottonwood Farms
17250 South Weber Road
Lockport, IL 60441
(815) 741-3467

The Great Michigan Pumpkin Weigh Off
Michael Huggins
P.O. Box 97
LaSalle, MI 48145
(734) 242-2475

North Carolina Weigh Off
Ron Johnson
236 Main Street
Mooresville, NC 28115
(704) 663-5533

Great Dixon Mayfair Weigh Off
Mike Green
1949 London Lane
Fairfield, CA 94533
(916) 678-4765

Great Western Lakes Weigh Off (WI)
Jack Marks
5579 Marks Road
Oconomowoc, WI 53066
(414) 567-9503

Port City Pumpkin Weigh Off
Joe Crisafulli
PO Box 308
Oswego, NY 13126
(315) 342-2200

Great Missouri Weigh Off
Carl Huffman
Greenleaf Gardens
199 North Hwy. 60
Republic, MO 65738
(417) 732-7855

Great South Dakota Weigh Off
Bill Hartman
1009 W. 26th Street, #4
Sioux Falls, SD 57105
(605) 331-3912

Great Central Lakes Weigh Off (MI)
Andy & Sunday Todosciuk
3131 South US 27
St. Johns, Ml 48879
(517) 224-6398

New England Pumpkin Weigh Off
Hugh Wiberg
445 Middlesex Avenue
Wilmington, MA 01887
(978) 658-5852

Great Central Wisconsin Pumpkin Weigh Off
John Weidman
703 S. Section St.
Nekoosa, WI 54457
(715) 886-4472

Great Morton Pumpkin Weigh Off
Mike Badgerow
415 W. Jefferson St.
Morton, IL 61550
(309) 263-2491

Canada

Ottawa-St.Lawrence Growers (ON)
Gus Saunders
7930 Bleeks Road
RR 2, Ashton, ON
KOA 1BO
(613) 838-5435

Great Southern Ontario Weigh Off
Fred Cooper
RR#1
Troy, ON
L0R 2B0
(519) 647-2714

Roland Pumpkin Fair (MB)
Jake Neufeld
Box 106, Roland, MB
ROG 1T0
(204) 343-2125

Sarnia Sunripe Rotary Weigh Off
Pete Geerts
6749 Nauveo Rd.
RR 1, Arkona, ON
NOM 1B0
(519) 849-6315

Great White North Pumpkin Fair (AB)
Barry Wood
Box 71
Bellis, AB
TOA OJO
(403) 636-2181

WPC (World Pumpkin Confederation)

WPC Headquarters
Ray Waterman
14050 Rt 62,
Collins, New York 14034 USA
Phone:(716)532-5995 FAX (716)532-5690, 24 HOURS.

Arizona Weigh Off at Mother Natures
Sam Kelsall, #160, 1110 E Missouri,
Phoenix AZ 85014
Phone:(602) 234 1999

Iowa Weigh Off
Fred Boer
407 Valleau
Sanbom, IA 51248
(712)729-3216.

Minnesota Weigh Off
Tom Tweite
Tweites' Mercantile
1821 Frontier Rd. SW,
Byron MN 55920
(507)365-8035

Illinois Weigh Off,
Flower Shop & Greenhouses
170 River Rd,
Des Plaines, IL
Chris Pesche
(847)299-1300

Tennessee - Weigh Off
James Asberry
P0 Box 10
Allardt, TN 38504
(615)879-9605

British National Pumpkin Society
Mike Turner
P.O. Box 524
Meriden
Coventry, England CV7 7ZU

BELGIUM Weigh Off
Rene Sterckx
Huldenbergstraat 24
B3080, Duisburg
ITALY Weigh Off
Roberto Franceschetti
Via Maspiano 59,
25057 Sale Marasino (BS) Italy

SWEDEN Weigh Off
Torbjorn Kerje
Valthornsvagen 31, 4tr
Uppsala, Sweden

Russia Weigh Off
Maxim Masharuev
Primorskaya St,
Bratsk 665709 Russia

IPA (International Pumpkin Association)
2155 Union St.
San Francisco, CA 94123
Contact: Terry Pimsleur

Independent Sites

Atlantic Pumpkin Growers
Danny Dill
PO Box 901
Windsor, NS, Canada
BON 2T0
(902)798-1082

Eastern States Exhibition
West Springfield, MA
(mid-September)

Half Moon Bay, CA

Giant Growers Association,
c/o Weeks Seed Co.
Raleigh, NC

Northern Tier Giant Pumpkin Club,
Northeastern, PA
(early October) 717-596-4414

Port Elgin Pumpkinfest
Jan Bonhomme
515 Goderich St.
Port Elgin, Ontario, Canada
N0H 2C4

Associations

Australia Giant Pumpkin Society
P.O. Box 7032
Karingal Centre
Victoria, 3199, Australia
Contact: Wendy Stayner

British National Pumpkin Society
P.O. Box 524
Meriden, Coventry, England CV7 7ZU
Contact: Mike Turner

Great Pumpkin Commonwealth
445 Middlesex Ave.
Wilmington, MA 01887
Contact: Hugh Wiberg

New England Pumpkin Growers Assn.
445 Middlesex Ave
Wilmington, MA 01887
Contact: Hugh Wiberg
(Quarterly Newsletter) $12/yr. US$

Ottawa/St. Lawrence Growers Asso.
7930 Bleeks Road, RR 2, Ashton, ON
KOA 1BO
Contact: Gus Saunders
(Quarterly Newsletter) $15/yr. US$,
$20/yr Canadian

Ohio Valley Giant Pumpkin Growers
4576 SR9
Salem, OH 44460
Contact: Alan Gibson
(Quarterly Newsletter) $20/yr. US$

Rhode Island Pumpkin Growers Asso.
42 Walker St.
Norton, MA 02766
Contact: Don Langevin
(Quarterly Newsletter) $10/yr. US$

Southern Pumpkin Growers Assn.
2913 Harrison Road
Falls Church, VA 22042
Contact: Joe Mills
(Semi-annual Newsletter) $20 yr. US$

World Pumpkin Confederation
14050 Rt 62,
Collins, New York 14034
Contact: Ray Waterman

Atlantic Giant Seed

United States

Annedawn Publishing,
Box 247, Norton, MA 02766
(800) 985-7878
Visa/Mastercard Accepted

P&P Seeds
14050 Gowanda State Road
Collins, NY 14034

Harris Seeds
P.O. Box 22960
Rochester, NY 14692

Gurney Seed & Nursery
110 Capital St.
Yankton, SD 57079

Henry Field's Seed & Nursery
415 N. Burnett
Shenandoah, IA 51602

J.W. Jung Seed Co.
335 South High St.
Randolph, WI 53957

Nichols Garden Nursery
1190 North Pacific Hwy. NE
Albany, OR 97321

Willhite Seed Inc.
P.O. Box 23
Poolville, TX 76487
Johnny's Selected Seeds
310 Foss Hill Rd.
Albion, ME 04910

Ed Hume Seed Inc.
P.O. Box 1450
Kent, WA 98032

Territorial Seed Company
P.O. Box 15, 20 Palmer Ave.
Cottage Grove, OR 97424

Earl May Seed & Nursery
208 N. Elm
Shenandoah, Iowa 51603
Osborne Intl. Seed Co.
1679 Highway 99 South
Mount Vernon, WA 98273

Pinetree Garden Seeds
P.O. Box, 616 A Lewiston Rd.
New Gloucester, ME04260

Siegers Seed Co.
8265 Felch St.
Zeeland,MI 49464

Canada

Howard Dill Enterprises
RR#1
Windsor, NS
Canada B0N 2T0

Vesey's Seed Ltd.
York, PEI
Canada C0A 1P0

Stokes Seed Ltd.
Box 10
St. Catherines, ON
Canada L2R 6R6

McKenzie Seed Co.
30 9th St.
Brandon, MB
Canada R7A 6N4

Ontario Seed Co. Ltd.
330 Philip St., Box 144
Waterloo, ON
Canada N2J 3Z9

Dominion Seed House
Box 2500
Georgetown, ON
Canada L7G 5L6

Halifax Seed Co.
5860 Kane St.
Halifax, NS
Canada B3K 5L8

Atlantic Giant ® is the registered
trademark of Howard Dill Enterprises.

Plantfood

EnP, Inc.
2001 Main Street
Box 618
Mendota, IL 61342

Neptune's Harvest
88 Commercial St.
Box 1183
Gloucester, MA 01930

North Country Organics
RR#1, Box 2232
Bradford, VT 05033

Nitron Organic Gardening Products
P.O. Box 1447
Fayetteville, AR 72702

Internet Web Sites and Message Board

WORLD CLASS GIANT PUMPKINS
http://www.athenet.net/~dang/pumpkins.html

OTTAWA-ST. LAWRENCE GROWERS
http://www.magi.com/~farmrgus/

ATLANTIC GIANT PUMPKINS
http://www.eskimo.com/~mcalpin/pumkin.html

PUMPKIN ARCHIVES AND LIST
http://www.mallorn.com/lists/pumpkins/

Message Board
majordomo@mallorn.net
Type "subscribe pumpkins [your email
address]" in the body of email. Leave
subject blank.

Videos

Holland's Land O' Giants
Joel and Mari Lou Holland
P.O. Box 969
Sumner, WA 98390

Al Berard of Sanford, ME provided these pictures of his 1997, 646.2-pounder which was officially weighed at the Topsfield Fair in Topsfield, MA.

#5
7/29/97

#5
8/3/97

#5
8/13/97

#5
8/28/97

#5
9/10/97

#5
10/3/97

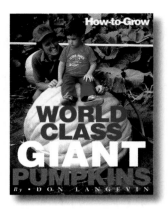

How-to-Grow World Class Giant Pumpkins
by Don Langevin
128 pages, 200 color photos
14.95 plus $4 shipping and handling

Considered to be the "bible" on growing giant pumpkins, this book put the average backyard gardener on a level playing field with the best giant pumpkin growers in the world. Published in 1993 and still considered the definitive text on the subject. Covers everything from A to Z. The perfect companion book to How-to-Grow World Class Giant Pumpkins, II.

How-to-Grow World Class Giant Pumpkins, II
by Don Langevin
160 pages, 250 color photos
17.95 plus $4 shipping and handling

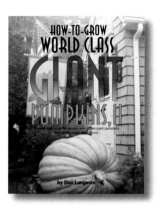

Totally updated with all new photos and illustrations. Contains new information, data and cultural practices, yet covers everything you need to know to grow a world record pumpkin. Great for both the experienced or new grower — a great companion for How-to-Grow World Class Giant Pumpkins.

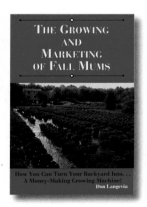

The Growing and Marketing of Fall Mums
by Don Langevin
228 pages, many photos and illustrations
16.95 plus $4 shipping and handling

Covers everything you need to know about growing prize winning fall mums for sale. Covers all aspects of growing and marketing your product — from securing cuttings and making your soil mix to pinching, feeding and profitably selling everything you grow. The only book of its kind. Thousands sold to new and experienced commercial growers. Start your backyard flower business today!

World Class Dill's Atlantic Giant Pumpkin Seeds
These seeds come from cross pollinations of heavy, top producing seed stocks.
Each packet marked with pumpkin weight and female x male cross.
7 seeds per packet for $5 (includes postage and handling).

To order books or seeds directly from Annedawn Publishing write to:
Annedawn Publishing, Box 247, Norton, MA 02766
or call 1-800-985-7878
Visa and Mastercard accepted.